Life Amid the Principalities

The Pro Ecclesia Series

Books in The Pro Ecclesia Series are "for the Church." The series is sponsored by the Center for Catholic and Evangelical Theology, founded by Carl Braaten and Robert Jenson in 1991. The series seeks to nourish the Church's faithfulness to the gospel of Jesus Christ through a theology that is self-critically committed to the biblical, dogmatic, liturgical, and ethical traditions that form the foundation for a fruitful ecumenical theology. The series reflects a commitment to the classical tradition of the Church as providing the resources critically needed by the various churches as they face modern and post-modern challenges. The series will include books by individuals as well as collections of essays by individuals and groups. The Editorial Board will be drawn from various Christian traditions.

OTHER TITLES IN THE SERIES INCLUDE:

- *The Morally Divided Body: Ethical Disagreement and the Disunity of the Church*, edited by Michael Root and James J. Buckley
- *Christian Theology and Islam*, edited by Michael Root and James J. Buckley
- *Who Do You Say That I Am? Proclaiming and Following Jesus Today*, edited by Michael Root and James J. Buckley
- *What Does It Mean to "Do This"? Supper, Mass, Eucharist*, edited by Michael Root and James J. Buckley
- *Heaven, Hell, . . . and Purgatory?*, edited by Michael Root and James J. Buckley

Life Amid the Principalities

Identifying, Understanding, and Engaging Created, Fallen, and Disarmed Powers Today

Edited by
Michael Root &
James J. Buckley

 CASCADE *Books* • Eugene, Oregon

LIFE AMID THE PRINCIPALITIES
Identifying, Understanding, and Engaging Created, Fallen, and Disarmed Powers Today

Pro Ecclesia Series 6

Copyright © 2016 Wipf and Stock Publishers. All rights reserved. Except for brief quotations in critical publications or reviews, no part of this book may be reproduced in any manner without prior written permission from the publisher. Write: Permissions, Wipf and Stock Publishers, 199 W. 8th Ave., Suite 3, Eugene, OR 97401.

Cascade Books
An Imprint of Wipf and Stock Publishers
199 W. 8th Ave., Suite 3
Eugene, OR 97401

www.wipfandstock.com

PAPERBACK ISBN: 978-1-4982-3721-5
HARDCOVER ISBN: 978-1-4982-3723-9
EBOOK ISBN: 978-1-4982-3722-2

Cataloguing-in-Publication data:

Names: Root, Michael, editor. | Buckley, James J., editor.

Title: Life amid the principalities : identifying, understanding, and engaging created, fallen, and disarmed powers today / edited by Michael Root and James J. Buckley.

Description: Eugene, OR : Cascade Books, 2016 | Pro Ecclesia Series

Identifiers: ISBN 978-1-4982-3721-5 (paperback) | ISBN 978-1-4982-3723-9 (hardcover) | ISBN 978-1-4982-3722-2 (ebook)

Subjects: LCSH: Powers (Christian theology)—Biblical teaching. | Bible. New Testament—Criticism, interpretation, etc.

Classification: BS2545.P663 L54 2016 (paperback) | BS2545.P663 L54 (ebook)

Manufactured in the U.S.A.   09/12/16

Contents

Contributors • vii
Preface • ix

1. The "Powers and Principalities": Problems and Prospects for Christian Doctrine Today • 1
   PAUL R. HINLICKY

2. The Powers and Paul's Letter to the Romans • 24
   BEVERLY ROBERTS GAVENTA

3. Does It Matter That Constantine Ended Sacrifice and Was Baptized? • 38
   VIGEN GUROIAN

4. Evil and the Principalities: Disarming the Demonic • 51
   CYNTHIA L. RIGBY

5. Augustine on Principalities and Powers • 68
   C. C. PECKNOLD

6. Christ and the Free Market • 81
   DANIEL M. BELL JR.

7. Technology as Principality: The Elimination of Incarnation • 99
   P. TRAVIS KROEKER

Contributors

Daniel M. Bell Jr. is Professor of Theology and Ethics at Lutheran Theological Southern Seminary in Columbia, South Carolina. He has authored several books, including *The Economy of Desire: Christianity and Capitalism in a Postmodern World* (2012) and *Just War as Christian Discipleship* (2009).

James J. Buckley is Professor of Theology at Loyola University Maryland. He is a member of the North American Lutheran Catholic dialogue and an associate director of the Center for Catholic and Evangelical Theology. He recently co-authored with Frederick Bauerschmidt *Catholic Theology: An Introduction* (Wiley Blackwell, 2017).

Beverly Roberts Gaventa is Distinguished Professor of New Testament at Baylor University as well as Helen H. P. Manson Professor *Emerita* of New Testament Literature and Exegesis at Princeton Theological Seminary. Her most recent publications include *Our Mother Saint Paul* (2007) and *Apocalyptic Paul*, an edited volume published by Baylor University Press (2013).

Vigen Guroian is Professor of Religious Studies in Orthodox Christianity at the University of Virginia. He is the author of numerous books, including *Incarnate Love: Essays in Orthodox Ethics* (2002), *The Melody of Faith: Theology in an Orthodox Key* (2010), and *Tending the Heart of Virtue: How Classic Stories Awaken a Child's Moral Imagination* (1998).

Paul R. Hinlicky is the Tise Professor of Lutheran Studies at Roanoke College; Professor of Systematic Theology at the Institute of Lutheran Theology; and Docent of the Protestant Theological Faculty, Comenius University, Bratislava. He is author of *Paths Not Taken*; *Luther and the Beloved Community*; *Divine Complexity*; *Before Auschwitz*; *Rethinking Philosophy* and *Theology with Deleuze* (with Brent Adkins); and *Beloved Community: Critical Dogmatics after Christendom*.

P. Travis Kroeker, Professor of Religious Studies at McMaster University in Hamilton, Ontario, is the author of *Christian Ethics and Political Economy in North America* (1995), and coauthor (with Bruce Ward) of *Remembering the End: Dostoevsky as Prophet to Modernity* (2001). Kroeker's current research interests include apocalyptic literature and political theology, and the relationship between immortality, ethics and political judgment in selected ancient and modern theologies. He is currently completing two book projects: *Messianic Political Theology and Diaspora Ethics* and *Literary Apocalypse as Political Theology*.

C. C. Pecknold, is Associate Professor of Theology at The Catholic University of America in Washington, DC. He is the author of *Transforming Postliberal Theology* (2005) and *Christianity and Politics: A Brief Guide to the History* (2010), as well as coeditor of *The T. & T. Clark Companion to Augustine and Modern Theology* (2014). He is currently writing a Catholic interpretation of Augustine's *City of God*.

Cynthia L. Rigby, an ordained minister of Word and Sacrament in the Presbyterian Church (USA), is the W. C. Brown Professor of Theology at Austin Presbyterian Theological Seminary in Austin, Texas. She holds the PhD and MDiv degrees from Princeton Theological Seminary and the AB from Brown University. An active member of the American Academy of Religion, she cochairs the Reformed Theology and History Group and is an associate editor for Brill's *Journal of Reformed Theology*. Rigby enjoys teaching in both ecclesial and academic settings. She is the author of *Promotion of Social Righteousness* (2010) and *Holding Faith* (2015). She is married to Bill Greenway, also a professor at Austin Seminary, and has two children: Xander, 11, and Jessica, 9.

Michael Root is Professor of Systematic Theology at The Catholic University of America and Executive Director of the Center for Catholic and Evangelical Theology. He was formerly the Director of the Institute for Ecumenical Research, Strasbourg, France.

Preface

"WE ARE NOT CONTENDING against flesh and blood, but against the principalities, against the powers, against the world rulers of this present darkness" (Eph 6:12). So Paul warns his Ephesian readers. And yet Paul also says that these principalities and powers were created in and for Christ (Col 1:16) and cannot separate us from the love of God (Rom 8:38). What are the principalities and powers of our time? How do we understand them as created, fallen, and disarmed? How does the Christian today engage these powers? These are the questions speakers and participants addressed at the 2014 conference of the Center for Catholic and Evangelical Theology.

The responses begin with Paul Hinlicky's theology of the principalities and Beverly Roberts Gaventa's study of the principalities in Paul's letter to the Romans. They continue through Vigen Guroian's challenge to Western (Catholic or Protestant) "Constantinian" readings of Christendom and Chad Pecknold's account of Augustine's traditional Latin version of the principalities. They conclude with three essays that focus on the principalities today: Cynthia Rigby on their bearing on contemporary discussion of evil, Daniel Bell on the free market as principalities, and P. Travis Kroeker on technology's elimination of incarnation as the embodiment of the principalities today and tomorrow.

Discussion among these Catholic (Anglo-, Orthodox, and Roman) and Evangelical (Anglo-, mainstream, and radical reformations) theologians produced some answers as well as challenges to our original questions. We invite readers of this volume to seek both the answers and the challenges as part of what we hope is a common effort to develop a Catholic and Evangelical theology.

Michael Root, Catholic University of America
James J. Buckley, Loyola University Maryland

1

The "Powers and Principalities"
Problems and Prospects for Christian Doctrine Today

Paul R. Hinlicky

In faith, we struggle against that which only truly becomes known in the light of Jesus Christ, and in the power of His Spirit, we likewise struggle for the Beloved Community of the Father.

THE BIBLICAL "SEAT OF doctrine" for our theme comes from the Letter to the Ephesians, "Our struggle is not against flesh and blood, but against the principalities, against the powers, against the world rulers of this present darkness, against the spiritual hosts of wickedness in the heavenly places" (Eph 6:12 RSV). As the epigraph indicates, however, this statement comes in the context of the early catholic development of Paul's evangelical theological legacy in the treatise we call Ephesians. These words come *after* the historical apostle's imminent expectation of the literal end of time had faded from view, that is to say, *with* the emergence of the church as the Spirit's good in its own right here and now, prefiguring, as it does, the victorious coming at the last of the Beloved Community of God. From this I derive a thesis for us today.

What we are to do as pastors and theologians of catholic and evangelical persuasion in struggle against the powers and principalities is to build up engaged and caring communities of Christ's people as knowing alternatives to the wicked lust for domination that animates the rebellious powers and principalities; these manifest as, and in the light of Jesus Christ we are to know and to name them as, structures of malice working injustice. As instrument of God's eschatological purpose and as a good in its own right (Eph 1:3–23), the renewing, realigning, and reuniting church emerging today from the ruins of Euro-American Christendom is to be built up as a structure of love working righteousness. In this new existence, the ecclesia will also serve as the stick that the Holy Spirit pokes into the spokes of the wheel (Bonhoeffer) of the unsustainable juggernaut on which Euro-America is being driven to catastrophe, be it ecological or economic if not already moral. Such ministry requires a kind of prophetic criticism of culture, far more insightful and penetrating than the borrowed bromides and bombast from our politics as usual that characterize political parties organized by greed and envy. We who are pastors and theologians in the Euro-American context are to understand that in the making and sustaining of holy community in Christ, locally and universally, we undertake the Spirit's holy struggle that protests the false choices of today's politics, even as the Spirit works finally to defeat forever the contra-divine powers.

In the space allotted, I can hardly argue this fulsome thesis, but only sketch the argument that I have made in my systematic theology[1] about the structures of malice working injustice within which and against which a post-Christendom church, evangelical and catholic, must arise on the soil of Euro-America to embody and so to witness in holy struggle the redemptive alternative of Beloved Community. Let me note here in passing, since I do not have time to explore it with the attention it deserves, that this struggle in our so-called First World context of Euro-American post-Christendom reflects some different cultural challenges than those confronting many of the younger churches, where, for pertinent instance, the powers and principalities show another face (2 Cor 11:14). Yet it is, per hypothesis, a common struggle against the very same spiritual forces of wickedness in high places here as there. The point is merely that we acknowledge the particularities

---

1. Paul R. Hinlicky, *Beloved Community: Critical Dogmatics after Christendom* (Grand Rapids: Eerdmans, 2015).

of our historical and cultural location in critical dogmatics. We in Euro-America live in the unprecedented situation of post-Christendom. This has not a little to do with the juggernaut that afflicts the Two-Thirds World. But we must—urgently, also for the sake of our afflicted sisters and brothers in the global South—attend to our own struggle.

In what follows, accordingly, I will spend the bulk of my effort, first, treating the welter of issues in our context that gives rise to my thesis and, second, I will attend to the significant objection to the thesis that is voiced both from within and from outside the churches, truth be told, in defense of the modern status quo ante: namely, an objection to the demonology of our text as a mystification. The objection maintains that the enlightened world with contemporary Euro-America at the helm, with its science and technology and virtual monopoly on the means of coercion, can and should set the agenda for the church. The result is that this "secular" order—the very one which *prima facie* Pauline theology regards as passé (1 Cor 7:31)—claims unqualified sovereignty: is to be built up as embodying the best possible justice available here and now.

As we shall see, my thesis does not simplistically contradict this secularism or merely invert its values. At least some of the powers can be reordered to serve the purposes of the coming divine sovereignty effected and made known in Jesus Christ. Thus, in conclusion, I will have something to say about political sovereignty and its divine mandate (Rom 13:1–7) and the vocation of the baptized within it, also here in Euro-America. This will differ[2] from the great contributions that Stanley Hauerwas[3] and his students have made to our theme (see the contribution of Daniel Bell to the present volume). Yet let me acknowledge with Hauerwas and his students that it is the proclaimed gospel in the Spirit's mission to the nations that sets the theological agenda, making the making and keeping of the church as holy community the *sine qua non* of the mission. But for the present thesis (Eph 1:20–22), this includes the church as the place of formation for the ministry of the people of God within political sovereignty despite all the anomalies and paradoxes that entails.[4] The result is a renewed mandate "to test the spirits to see whether they are from God" (1 John 4:1), a task of

2. Steffen Lösel, "The *Kirchenkampf* of the Countercultural Colony: A Critical Response," *Theology Today* 67 (2010) 279–98.

3. Stanley Hauerwas and William H. Willimon, *Resident Aliens: Life in the Christian Colony*, expanded 25th anniversary ed. (Nashville: Abingdom, 2014).

4. Reinhold Niebuhr, *Moral Man and Immoral Society: A Study in Ethics and Politics* (New York: Scribner's, 1960); *The Irony of American History* (New York: Scribner's, 1952).

discernment that I term "critical dogmatics." In conclusion, I will lay out a set of theological conditions for making the difficult notion of the contra-divine powers intelligible in our context that meet the aforementioned objection to mystification.

The holy Christian struggle is articulated in doctrine for life, not doctrine for doctrine, that is, theoretical speculation that seeks to transcend the apocalyptic battle in which we are placed by the coming of the Spirit through the gospel.

In his influential and well-intended books of the past generation, *Naming the Powers* and *Engaging the Powers*,[5] Walter Wink has argued that Pauline powers and principalities ambiguously denote *both* "human/institutional" *and* "spiritual" powers,[6] and thus are to be taken together as simultaneous aspects of "one concretion of power." Logically considered, this latter is, plainly, a non sequitur. It does not follow that if two things appear confusedly or ambiguously as one thing that this appearance is one thing. It does not follow that if the state, for example, appears as Stalin's Gulag that the state is gulag. The basic contention of Wink that Paul's language has wide scope so that under it one should critically consider and theologically evaluate all claims for an authoritative principle of origin and/or for lordship with power liberating and vengeful, I think, has withstood scholarly scrutiny.[7] But the other proposal of Wink, that human institution and demonic spiritual power form one concretion of power, has been subjected to, as it seems to me, withering exegetical and hermeneutical criticism.[8]

More broadly, as we shall see, the idea that the devil can be named and engaged concretely as some evident social formation— say, as capitalism or as communism, as patriarchy or as the present anarchy of the sexual

---

5. Walter Wink, *Naming the Powers: The Language of Power in the New Testament* (Philadelphia: Fortress, 1984); *Engaging the Powers: Discernment and Resistance in a World of Domination* (Minneapolis: Fortress, 1992).

6. So also Chris Forbes, "Paul's Principalities and Powers: Demythologizing Apocalyptic?," *Journal for the Study of the New Testament* 23 (2001) 61–88.

7. Chris Forbes, "Pauline Demonology and/or Cosmology? Principalities, Powers and the Elements of the World in Their Hellenistic Context," *Journal for the Study of the New Testament* 24 (2002) 51–73.

8. Chloe Lynch, "How Convincing Is Walter Wink's Interpretation of Paul's Language of the Powers?," *Evangelical Quarterly* 83 (2011) 251–66. Fellow evangelical theologian Gerald McDermott has argued from a different angle for the non-reducible reality of the principalities and powers as "other real supernatural powers besides God" in his *God's Rivals: Why Has God Allowed Different Religions? Insights from the Bible and the Early Church* (Downers Grove, IL: IVP Academic, 2007) 67–83.

revolution—contravenes the intention of the Ephesians text. The text rather wants to *distance* the spiritual powers of wickedness in high places from such human-all-too-human demonizing of earthly opponents; it wants to provide an insight into a true conflict behind the scenes, as is the wont of the apocalyptic genre; it does so in order to specify precisely what is new and redemptive about the action of God in Christ by the Spirit, namely, the holy struggle to make and keep a new polity in the world that is the ecclesia. Here the spiritual power of God's righteousness on the earth is to be sought and found, not in politics as usual (Mark 10:35–45). We should follow these intentions of the text, at least if we wish to be justified in deploying its revelation of struggle for holiness and against the demonic forces as a warrant in theology today.

Moreover, I have to add, any theologian today who thinks, as I do, in the tradition of Luther must surely and with unreserved self-critical force repudiate that great man's great sin of demonizing opponents, as I spelled out in the appendix to *Luther and the Beloved Community*.[9] Disastrously, Luther came to see one demonic concretion of power in the human institution of papacy, and, in the same vein, in the flesh-and-blood fellows who were angry peasants and the exotic rabbinic scholars. Indulging himself with verbal violence in manifest violation of his own Reformatory principle that the true people of God are they who bring to bear the judgment of the cross upon themselves,[10] Luther did not follow the intention of the Ephesians text patiently to bear with evident opponents, as per Prof. Daniel Bell's wonderful turn of phrase, in the "refusal to cease suffering."[11] Such patiency with others, even apparent enemies, is the point of affirming that our true struggle is *not* with flesh and blood.

Having announced the differentiation I intend to urge against Wink, I hasten to lift up, as previously with Hauerwas' work, the significant contribution his studies have made: naming and engaging the powers in holy struggle is an inalienable aspect of the ministry of the gospel that we discard at our own peril. We are not done with the powers when we discard them as illusory remnants from the prescientific past; rather, we become their enlightened pawns, all the more blinded because of the light we now

---

9. Paul R. Hinlicky, *Luther and the Beloved Community: A Path for Christian Theology after Christendom* (Grand Rapids: Eerdmans, 2010) 379–85.

10. Heiko A. Oberman, *The Roots of Anti-Semitism in the Age of Renaissance and Reformation*, trans. James I. Porter (Philadelphia: Fortress, 1984).

11. Daniel M. Bell Jr., *Liberation Theology after the End of History: The Refusal to Cease Suffering* (London: Routledge, 2001).

have. In any event, the theology of the powers and principalities is, if it is anything, instruction for *battle*. Wink has rightly seen this and made the theological problem of Christian demonology acute again wherever the New Testament is read and heard as Scripture.

Indeed, as every preacher who strives to be faithful to New Testament texts quickly discovers, whatever the ontology, she cannot tell the gospel narrative apart from that uncanny figure of malice, the devil.[12] That this rhetorical necessity creates profound problems of intelligibility is, of course, true; indeed, it accounts for the tendency in Wink's work softly to demythologize, so to say, the spiritual forces of wickedness into the human institutions they captivate as that "one concretion of power" of which he speaks. I will turn to that acute problem of intelligibility later on. But, for the moment, the point is that we are today indebted to Wink, who has rightly lifted up the holy struggle against the spiritual forces of wickedness in high places as the *raison d'être* of the theology of the powers in today's world where progress in science and technology has not ended institutional violence but all the more powerfully equipped it, indeed *entrenched* it.

Predominantly, however, the received theological tradition is marked by a tendency other than the Ephesians text's summons that we, here on the earth, struggle in the Spirit against the spiritual forces of wickedness. It has articulated angelology as a more or less disciplined speculation about the cosmic harmonies hidden beyond the veil of earthly conflict and confusion. In justified curiosity about our text's intimation that phenomenal appearances of merely human, purely social struggle do not tell the whole story, the tradition is thus tempted either to overlook the crucial assumption the Ephesians text makes, namely, that the Christian life is a *social* one ("*our* struggle") against forces of *malice*. Or it misconstrues the sense of this struggle as one of the individual's ascetic ascent from the earthly realm to a heavenly one, cognitively, then, beyond the "deformed imagery used by scripture in regard to the angels."[13] Imagining a celestial world of pure harmony behind the earthly veil of evident conflict in the Neoplatonic speculations of his *Celestial Hierarchy*, Pseudo-Dionysius thus overlooked

---

12. Dennis Bielfeldt et al., *The Substance of the Faith: Luther's Doctrinal Theology for Today* (Minneapolis: Fortress, 2008) 174–89.

13. *Pseudo-Dionysius: The Complete Works*, trans. Colm Luibheid (New York: Paulist, 1987) 153. We owe to Platonism both the great mandate to think critically by distinguishing appearance and reality and the sub-Christian tendency to locate the source of human sin in individuation and embodiment. By this we divinize mind and demonize body. Platonism must be far more critically received than in Pseudo-Dionysius.

the *militancy* of the Spirit who makes holy war against the flesh, as the usual Pauline idiom has it. As a consequence, Pseudo-Dionysius construes the Pauline conflict as one of overcoming earth-bound sensuality and passions to attain to the passionlessness of angelic existence, as he imagines it.[14] This is simply *not* the struggle of the ecclesia on the earth for an embodied righteousness, as our Ephesians text projects.

Deplatonizing Paulinism in favor of apocalyptic as the "mother of Christian theology" (Käsemann)—to mention one of the previously criticized Luther's abiding contributions—we should know that the Pauline conflict between the Spirit and the flesh is the conflict between reliance on the God who has come to us in Jesus Christ by the Spirit's preaching of the gospel and creaturely reliance on its own brainpower or muscle-power to do what this God alone can do and does for creatures. It is thus a struggle of faith, over what is first of all and over all to be trusted, believed, obeyed, hoped and loved with ultimate concern. Precisely when we recall and hold fast to that usual Pauline way of speaking, our theme text makes the crucial clarification about this holy militancy as the struggle to believe the God of the gospel rather than idols and demons, indeed, positively to disbelieve the idols and demons (as I learned many years ago now from my *Doktorvater*, Christopher Morse[15]). Christians do not struggle with swords of steel or, more subtly, with the verbal violence of political propaganda against fellow human beings similarly armed in the usual contests in the *libido dominandi* of this present age. But by the Word of God and in the mode of critical thinking that tests the spirits Christians struggle against supra-individual, trans-human forces of incorrigible *wickedness*. To know *this* enemy is not a matter of ordinary observation or curious speculation; it is a matter of learning God by the coming into the world of the One sent to break into the strong man's house to bind him and plunder his goods (Mark 3:27). It is revealed knowledge, not least, because that strong man fights back. "What

---

14. This judgment does not express in the first place a Lutheran judgment on Eastern Orthodoxy, but an Orthodox self-critique. See ch. 3, "The Origenist Crisis of the Sixth Century," and ch. 5, "Pseudo-Dionysius," in John Meyendorff, *Christ in Eastern Christian Thought* (Crestwood, NY: St. Vladimir's Seminary Press, 1975) 47–68, 91–111. It does, however, correspond to Luther's considered opinion. Mickey L. Mattox, "The Ordered Cosmos: The Mediation of God's Word in the Midst of Conflict" (unpublished paper) explores Luther's critical reception of the Dionysian cosmological speculation along these lines.

15. Christopher Morse, *Not Every Spirit: A Dogmatics of Christian Disbelief* (Harrisburg, PA: Trinity Press International, 1994).

have you to do with us, Jesus of Nazareth? Have you come to destroy us? I know who you are, the Holy One of God!" (Mark 1:24).

In our Western tradition, as John Milbank's seminal book has taught us,[16] contemporary sociology is the secular offspring of the Christian theology of the powers and principalities in that it apprehends the social and historical modes of organized life on the earth that form the human mind with mandates, rituals and final purposes, whether anyone is conscious or not of these supervening social forces. Insofar as it describes these as *heavenly* forces of *wickedness*, however, our text does not permit the common contemporary sociological reduction to impersonal structures that we, as scientifically informed social engineers, might tweak with better public policy or more radically transform by revolutionary action. Social structures can be wisely or stupidly designed; they can be anachronistically maintained or helpfully modernized, but they cannot per se sin. Only persons, human or otherwise, can sin. Structures can be sinful, then, in that persons maliciously organize themselves and other persons into structures of injustice. (Think, for recent and concrete example, of the Wall Street manipulators who cynically bet on massive mortgage defaults five years ago and thus nearly brought the entire global economy into a catastrophic depression. Think of the ensuing politics that then bailed out these sinners as too big to fail rather than question the injustice and reform the structure that enabled and indeed actualized such abuse.)

From the radical Christian theological perspective of the Apostle Paul, however, that judgment will fall in varying ways and degrees on *any* and indeed *all* social formation that exists in the spirit of self-reliance rather than in reliance of the Spirit on the heavenly Father who gave His Son precisely for such blind and bound sinners. Thus, our text speaks of structures of malice working an injustice so profound and comprehensive that apart from the Holy Spirit's intervention through the gospel we are in the dark, blind to the wickedness that is going on over us but also in us; so powerful is its grip on our own interiority in captivating our desire that apart from the breaking of Jesus Christ into our captivity by the gospel we cannot be freed or even want truly to be freed. Thinking of the Gospel of Mark's opening depiction of Jesus's battle with the demons, we might round out the apocalyptic picture this way: as the *Holy* Spirit falls upon Jesus in the river Jordan to send Him forth from the waters to do battle with the

---

16. John Milbank, *Theology and Social Theory: Beyond Secular Reason* (Oxford: Blackwell, 1997).

unclean spirits who captivate mere flesh and blood, so also those baptized by the same Spirit into the crucified but now vindicated Jesus Christ take up their crosses and just so rise up in new lives of holy *struggle*, following their liberating Lord whom they meet anew right back in workaday Galilee, the site of battle.

Do we so struggle? Do we meet Jesus in Galilee? Do we struggle so to preach and teach and thus lead others in this holy Christian struggle? Or do we flee from battle? On the dubious assumption that these dangerous biblical images of militant struggle—properly interpreted, to be sure, as in our Ephesians text—incline us to religious violence and hatred of the other, my denomination's recent hymnal rigorously censors out any and all language of the struggle that once structured Christian self-understanding as the Spirit's holy war against the world, the devil and our sinful selves.[17] As a systematic theologian who thinks, well, systematically, I fail to see how the Lutheran tribal anthem, "Ein Feste Burg ist Unser Gott," survived this purge; but it did (no doubt for a combination of reasons: sentimentality, marketability and useful pretext for continuing the habitual anti-Catholic smear). As a surd, then, erstwhile Lutherans still sing about hordes of devils filling the land, eager to devour us, until a champion of God's own choosing enters the field to win the victory on their behalf. Presumably, as a result, at least several times a year otherwise peaceable Lake Woebegoners empty from the churches itching for a fight. Surely "Children of the Heavenly Parent" would be the better choice for Hymn of the Day.

More seriously, with this shallow anthropology and ham-fisted social engineering, we move away from the creative ferment that comes from the recovery today of Paul's christologically modified apocalyptic theology[18] in exchange for the thin gruel of liberal Protestant progressivism *redivivus* with its "stillborn God," as Columbia University professor Mark Lilla so acutely diagnoses in his timely analysis of the modern separation of religion and politics in secular, "democratic" regimes. Lilla's brief, to be sure, is against the recurring outbreaks of christologically *unmodified* apocalyptic theology, as in crusades, inquisitions, and wars of religion, where demonizing opponents lends political conflict an unmanageable fanaticism and intractable dogmatism. "Liberal theology began in rational hope [of Kant],

---

17. See the analysis of Sarah Hinlicky Wilson, "Peace, Peace, When There Is No Peace," *Lutheran Forum* 42 (2008) 3–6.

18. *Apocalyptic and the Future of Theology: With and Beyond J. Louis Martyn*, ed. Joshua B. Davis and Douglas Harink (Eugene OR: Cascade, 2012).

not fevered dreams. Its moderate wish was that the moral truths of biblical faith be intellectually reconciled with, and not just accommodated to, the realities of modern political life [separating church and state institutionally]. Yet the liberal deity turned out to be a stillborn God, unable to inspire genuine conviction among those seeking ultimate truth. For what did the new Protestantism offer to the soul of one seeking union with his creator? It prescribed a catechism of moral commonplaces and historical optimism about bourgeois life, spiced with deep pessimism about the possibility of altering that life."[19] Lilla thus wistfully describes, I venture, exactly where most of us tired Euro-American Christians are at today, especially in the old Protestant denominations. There is no change we believe in. We are the end of history. And we acquiesce to renditions, waterboarding, government spying on citizens and predator drone strikes to keep it that way.

Even if my denomination thinks itself progressive in returning to the theology of the nineteenth century to preach Lilla's "stillborn God," Christians have long known from Paul that we are living in a fragile place, a bubble about to burst, an interregnum, an interlude between the coming of the Messiah in the flesh and His Parousia. "In the now time," as post-Marxist philosopher Giorgio Agamben translates Paul's Greek,[20] the Spirit by the Word is engaged in struggle for hearts and minds in calling and sustaining the Beloved Community, Augustine's *civitas Dei*, breaking in by the Word concerning Christ crucified to bind the strong man and redeem his captives. Apocalypse now! Freed in this way, Christians have known that this "now time" is the time of the struggle of the Spirit through the Word against the contra-divine powers of sin, death, and devil, a time for witness, a time of confessing Jesus as Lord in a world awash with crises and corresponding messages of liberation, as may be seen, for instance, in the Little Apocalypse of Mark 13.

As commentator Joel Marcus has it, "If Mark 13:22 ["False messiahs and false prophets will appear and produce signs and omens, to lead astray, if possible, the elect"] is taken seriously, the majority of the Markan Christians will be enmeshed in the realm of demonic delusion—perhaps not only a tendency to follow false Christs (13:22) but also a related propensity to despair over the return of the true one (cf. 4:38, 6:48 . . .)." But

---

19. Mark Lilla, *The Stillborn God: Religion, Politics, and the Modern West* (New York: Vintage, 2007) 301.

20. Giorgio Agamben, *The Time That Remains: A Commentary on the Letter to the Romans*, trans. Patricia Dailey (Stanford: Stanford University Press, 2005).

The "Powers and Principalities"

the true Messiah by his passion and death on the cross has already fulfilled the prophecies of the end time in Mark 13: "The elect fall asleep (14:37, 40-41) and go astray (14:50-52, 66-72), the sun is dimmed (15:33), the temple suffers damage that portends its destruction (15:38), and the Son of Man passes through an all-night vigil until finally, on the other side of cosmic death, he returns as the herald of new life and a new age."[21] "Apocalypse now" comes by the gospel that reveals the crucified One as the Son of God or does not reveal Him at all, beginning such judgment within the household of God. Apocalypse now comes, not as the literal end of time so much as the time of the End breaking into the strong man's house. Christians therefore may struggle too, holy if so liberated to follow their Lord in bearing their own crosses, not only against the external world but even also within the church, *semper reformanda*, because their Lord has already struggled, pioneering the way, winning the victory. In His light and His truth as the *crucified* Messiah (1 Cor 2:2), they know the holy way forward (Luke 22:24-27)—true progress and Christian progressivism, if you will.

This, then, is what is revealed "in the now time"—not the literal "end of time" but the "time of the End" pressing in by the Spirit through the Word—under the name and knowledge of "theology of powers and principalities": there are many so-called gods and lords; they have no real existence (1 Cor 8:4-6; Jer 10:1-10) other than the mysterious forces of wickedness in higher places that make use of them (1 Cor 10:14, 21) to oppose the coming of God's reign, the Beloved Community of God. Their time draws near; the bubble is about to burst; the demons are flushed from their hiding places in direct proportion to the Spirit's coming by the gospel. In such times, the demons fight back: counterfeit revelations abound and urgent imperatives sound: "Lo! Here is the Messiah"—or, "There!" We hear new gospels telling us what must be done to save the situation: technological imperatives, market imperatives, imperatives to maximize personal freedom or social equality, imperatives for revolutionary praxis or sectarian separation from this dying world. This list of urgent calls to saving action could be multiplied, each registering intensity in direct proportion to the impending sense of crisis, yet in sorry truth each expressing only some immanent aspect of the common predicament rather than resolving it definitively, as each one falsely claims.

---

21. Joel Marcus, *Mark: A New Translation with Introduction and Commentary*, Anchor Bible 27A (New Haven: Yale University Press, 2009) 2:922-23.

Woe, then, to all who actually fall for such would-be "final solutions"![22] What then? For those with eyes open and ears alert among our contemporaries—I would especially lift up and recommend the aforementioned Agamben—the Euro-American bubble is about to burst. Here the philosopher appears as biblical prophet. Have we ears to hear? In this situation, we will rebuild engaged and caring communities of Christ's people by penetrating criticism of this culture that interprets the impending experience of the end of our comfortable world of affluence better than the usual alternatives—which have no solutions but offer only more of the same (more government spending, more economic growth, more, more, more . . . the politics of insatiable greed at war with insatiable envy).

Such penetrating prophetic criticism of ideology was the vision in 1964 of Harvard professor Amos Wilder, who described the recovery of the biblical kerygma in its eschatological dimension—what I previously termed "christologically modified apocalyptic" (Mark 14:33–39) that proclaims, in J. Louis Martyn's striking words, the cross of the Messiah as "the best of news in a still unredeemed world."[23] Wilder called this recovery an "exhilarating" rediscovery of "the deepest levels of Christian understanding . . . [with] momentous insights and affirmations" for articulating a timely Christian social ethic.[24] A brief extraction from this rich but forgotten essay permits me to bring this first part of my presentation to a conclusion in that it specifies the kind of *holy struggle* in which today we are to engage in battle with the principalities and powers.

In the aftermath of Hitler, Hiroshima, and Stalin, Wilder wrote of an "almost unparalleled demand upon the Church for ethical guidance. Those same totalitarian pressures which have forced Christians to clarify their faith and its biblical ground, have similarly compelled them to search the Scriptures for light on fundamental decisions as to the nature and limit of the State, the political witness of the believer and ultimate questions as to the relations of the Church and world." In want of such guidance, however, "many modern men with important responsibilities in society have

---

22. Paul R. Hinlicky, *Before Auschwitz: What Christian Theology Must Learn from the Rise of Nazism* (Eugene, OR: Cascade, 2013) 14–43.

23. J. Louis Martyn, "Epistemology at the Turn of the Ages: 2 Corinthians 5:16," in *Christian History and Interpretation: Studies Presented to John Knox*, ed. W. R. Farmer et al. (Cambridge: Cambridge University Press, 1967) 269–87.

24. A. N. Wilder, "Kerygma, Eschatology and Social Ethics," in *The Background of the New Testament and Its Eschatology: Studies in Honour of C. H. Dodd*, ed. W. D. Davies and D. Daube (Cambridge: Cambridge University Press, 1964) 509.

The "Powers and Principalities"

despaired of finding clear light for conduct and policy in the Bible, whether as regards law, politics, business, labour, marriage or property. In absence of such light they turn to secular moral philosophy or the great rival views of man which today oppose themselves to the Gospel, or, in private dilemmas, to a secular psychiatry or some esoteric cult." But "if we put at the center of our Christian message the theme that God has visited and redeemed his people, that in the Cross God dethroned the powers which hold men in bondage, that in the redeemed community there is neither Jew nor Greek, slave nor free, male nor female, black nor white, but all are one in Jesus Christ..." a genuine and timely engagement with the powers becomes possible today. Drawing on Barth, Bonhoeffer, and Bultmann (though critical of Bultmann's existential reduction to the individual's decision of faith that eclipses the social dimension of corporate faith), Wilder especially lifted up the problem of the Church's biblical-prophetic role of "watchman" over the city and the nations, asking how "aggressive" this guardianship is to be.[25]

That is perhaps a misleading formulation. The question is not about degrees of aggressiveness, but whether Christian cultural criticism accomplishes the Spirit's work "to prove the world wrong about sin and righteousness and judgment" (John 16:8). This is a "spiritual" battle, a battle *of the spirits*, addressing *conscience*. Christologically modified apocalyptic does not think, as does modern secularism in either its capitalist or socialist modes, of a battle of human spirit against indifferent nature, in the process liberating natural self-love from considerations of conscience and transforming natural envy and greed into positive motives for human action. "Flesh" for Paul designates humanity, not in its base animal emotions or motives but in its highest, "spiritual" powers, brain-power no less than muscle-power. Flesh is the spirit of self-reliance over against reliance on the Spirit of Jesus and His Father. The biblical battle is a battle of spirit against spirit. Thus prophetic critique in the Spirit is not to be measured by its level of "aggression," but by its capacity to lighten our darkness with a critique that necessitates the crucified Messiah as the God's forward to the Beloved Community of God (Gal 2:21).

Wilder does better in answering his own question. He notes that "no political authority in the ancient world was devoid of religious and metaphysical connotations," so that "the hostile rulers and angelic powers in question include transparently what we would speak of in non-mythological terms as structural elements of unregenerate society, the false

---

25. Ibid., 515.

authorities of culture." While this formulation is still too vague and we have to question, with Milbank, whether or not our modern sociological way of thinking is as demystified and non-mythological at it claims, Wilder derived from this basic insight the important mandate for theology: "The dethroning of such authorities and the weakening of such power-principles constitute the central task of Christian social action."[26] That is to say: the central social-ethical task is *public preaching* and theological reflection that makes such proclamation precise, pertinent, and powerful in destabilizing the metaphysical, or more precisely, the *soteriological* claims of political sovereignty.[27]

I take from this the important insight that Christian social action is anything but mute; it is public and articulate kerygma and liturgy and works of mercy (cf. 2 Cor 10:4) that as such and only as such contests the thralldom and wins hearts and minds to the Beloved Community by liberating them from idols and demons. Who, so to say, gets to demythologize who? Who, indeed, sets the agenda? Unlike Barth (though he does not mention it), yet following Paul, Wilder realizes that the reconciliation of the world to God in Christ is incomplete, that battle still rages, that the coming Christ in glory still has work to do in subduing the powers, that last of which is Death—a power, let me emphasize, to be *destroyed* (the Greek verb is *katargeo*) like Sin—*not* reconciled or reordered (1 Cor 15:26)—"death of death and hell's destruction," as we used to sing ("Guide Us, O Thou Great Jehovah").

In this light, today's contextual theologies are not wrong, as we see in Wink, to demand that we name and engage the powers here on earth, now in this situation of dire need; but who names who and how we so identified are to engage in a struggle that is *holy*, not more of the same old violence, is for Paul, and should be for us, a matter of knowing the sovereign work of the Spirit who is holy. This Spirit is the One who proclaims the crucified Jesus as Lord to the glory of the Father who sent Him, even to us undeserving. This Spirit's final horizon consists in nothing less than the defeat of Death, that "death of death and hell's destruction." The sovereignty of the Spirit of Jesus and His Father entails, accordingly, this firm specification of the politics of gospel: the gospel forms holy communities of Christ the crucified but vindicated Lord to whom at last every knee will bow when Death

---

26. Ibid., 528.

27. Robert W. Bertram, *A Time for Confessing*, ed. Michael Hoy, Lutheran Quarterly Books (Grand Rapids: Eerdmans, 2008).

is forever swallowed up in Life, provided only that in the interim this new existence of the ecclesia in the world is not mute but itself proclaimed and understood as the divine alternative to the politics of the *libido dominandi*.

The Problem of Intelligibility

If the foregoing discussion succeeds in its modest purpose of fleshing out what is at issue in the thesis that dethroning the powers comes by the formation of the church in the Spirit's gospel mission to the nations, we are confronted with an immediate and formidable objection. This is not an objection to the mixed record of Christianity in its two thousand years of history, as for contemporary example, Ephraim Radner has so acutely analyzed.[28] Nothing human, including the church, has other than a mixed historical record; as Augustine knew, precisely as a Catholic Christian, in this life our righteousness consists for the most part in the forgiveness of sins. Thus the only true problem in this regard is triumphalist resistance to acknowledging penitently the sinfulness of the church.[29] Rather, the salient objection in connection with our theme does not stem from within the church, properly considered, though in the churches it finds many notable exponents today. It stands behind Bultmann's existential reduction of the mythology of the powers and principalities to the individual's decision of faith to which Wilder took exception; it stands as well behind the softer demythologizing in Wink to human political and institutional powers that are to be identified as demonic in his "one concretion of power." But this objection at its root stems from a Feuerbach or a Durkeim who would expose the theological thesis about spiritual forces of wickedness in heavenly places as a mystification. And indeed, it is the case that we are now confronted with an acute problem of interpretation to which I alluded at the outset but set aside, namely, that according to our text appearances do not tell the whole story, or perceive the true roots of its apparent conflicts, and accordingly settle for a salvation less than the Pauline eschatological defeat of the trans-individual, supra-human apocalyptic powers of Sin and Death.

The distinction between appearance and reality is, of course, the basis of critical thinking. Theology too is a form of critical thinking. If differs

---

28. Ephraim Radner, *A Brutal Unity: The Spiritual Politics of the Christian Church* (Waco, TX: Baylor University Press, 2012).

29. See my response to Radner: Paul R. Hinlicky, "On the 'Sacrifice of Conscience,'" *Syndicate: A New Forum for Theology* 1/1 (2014) 11–17.

from philosophy in holding that epistemic access to the root conflict of human experience is not available to what Paul calls "the natural man" (1 Cor 2:14), but rather must rather be apocalypsed, revealed. If for a Feuerbach or a Durkheim, however, the very notion of God, let alone the revealing God of the Bible, is already a mystification of purely human-social aspiration, how much more so, then, must the notion of contra-divine powers be a mystification of human conflicts and struggles! Marx put it famously in speaking of religion as the opiate of the people. As Nietzsche said about the forgiveness of sins—an imaginary solution to an imaginary problem—so we might also say about sin, death, and devil as apocalyptic powers: an imaginary problem evoking an imaginary solution.

I admit to having at least a little sympathy with Feuerbach or Durkheim in this regard. When I was a college student in the Midwest years ago, a blizzard was predicted for the day of our travel back east for Christmas break. We respectfully asked our excessively pious dean for permission to take an exam early in order to drive in advance of the storm. Despite our pleas, our "all in good order" dean wouldn't violate the sacrosanct rules and grant our request for an exception. His parting words in all seriousness advised us to call upon the holy angels for protection, assuring us that if we prayed they would ride shotgun on all four fenders to keep us safe. The dean's appeal to the holy angels, like the "Devil made me do it" of the superstitious preacher's wife Geraldine in Flip Wilson's comedy routine—such are indeed mystifications that evade ethical responsibility, that maintain order at the expense of love and law at the expense of wisdom, and that invoke mystery to conceal muddles in thinking. Conversely, such mythologizing surrenders agency and makes victimhood a badge of personal identity: "I was only following orders." Christian theology of the powers and principalities today cannot go forward without wholehearted acceptance of the Enlightenment's critique of such superstitious mystification. But the Christian point of this is not so much to demythologize as to render all flesh accountable to God for that to which their hearts cling in every time of trouble.

Having acknowledged that, we also acknowledge after the enlightened century of Hitler, Hiroshima, and Stalin that the Enlightenment tradition suffers with its own superstitions and mystifications. As theologians we must go forward with the intention of the Ephesians text for today, which, as mentioned, is to deliteralize the Christian metaphors of military struggle by removing them from the human plane of politics as usual, where, as

The "Powers and Principalities"

history shows, Christians too can readily be misled into the bloody fanaticism of crusades, witch-hunts, persecutions and inquisitions, captured too by the lust for domination that always animates the struggle for power in politics as usual, whether by the Religious Right or the Religious Left. Again, as mentioned, the intention of the Ephesians text is to direct us to the ecclesia as the Spirit's new community in the world where politics are not to be as usual, just so, providing the alternative to structures of malice working injustice. Needless to say, this thesis implies a thoroughgoing realignment in the churches in order to align the holy remnant in Euro-America's ruins of Christendom. Here is a practical test of such fresh Christian theology of the powers and principalities: it should trump the Enlightenment's abiding challenge that devil talk amounts to a mystification of what is really going on by displaying a critical power of insight that out-enlightens the enlighteners (as Oswald Bayer has suggested in his interesting study of Hamann[30]).

But to meet the objection substantively, we have to ask: what in the world are we actually talking about when, in the light of Jesus Christ, we expose what we name and engage here on the earth as manifestations of the powers and principalities? That is the *crux intellectum*. It confronts every preacher every time she is required to make intelligible to her audience the kinds of biblical texts we have considered in this presentation. If this presentation is at all on target, moreover, we cannot give a glib answer to this question, for we have learned that the powers and principalities are a revealed mystery, that they disguise themselves as angels of light, that they are masters of deceit at work with super-human cunning. What is revealed, in other words, is the *mystery* of evil (2 Thess 2:7). Entering into this *mystery* for understanding is thus a matter of ongoing discernment. In conclusion, I am going to suggest that biblical texts that figure Satan in various guises give consideration to this *mystery*, and that just this consideration makes these texts about powers and principalities intelligible, so far as the *mystery of evil* can be made intelligible at all.

A lot of contemporary theological thinking based on responsible biblical scholarship,[31] but insufficiently hermeneutical and systematic

---

30. Oswald Bayer, *A Contemporary in Dissent: Johann Georg Hamann as a Radical Enlightener*, trans. Roy A. Harrisville and Mark C. Mattes (Grand Rapids: Eerdmans, 2012).

31. E.g., Anathea E. Portier-Young, *Apocalypse against Empire: Theologies of Resistance in Early Judaism* (Grand Rapids: Eerdmans, 2011). The continuity of Christian theology with its "mother," anti-imperial Jewish apocalyptic, is qualified by the *unexpected* cross of the Messiah, as the manner by which the heavenly powers and principalities

in method, seeks a different kind of intelligibility, along the lines of the soft, but finally incoherent demythologizing proposed by Wink. This work suggests that under the "code language" of the principalities and powers we are talking about empire, about imperialism. The most sophisticated contemporary advocate of this view is N. T. Wright.[32] In my view, however, this thesis has been decisively qualified, both methodologically and substantively, by John M. G. Barclay.[33]

In his *Auseinandersetzung* with Wright, Barclay articulates the thesis that "Paul's gospel is subversive of Roman imperial claims precisely by not opposing them within their own terms" since "even turning Roman values on their head entails a kind of confinement within the ideological system in which those values are defined."[34] "Opposing them within their own terms" is precisely what happens when we demythologize the powers and principalities by reducing this reference to the mystery of evil to the mere fact of *imperium*, as if short of the eschaton there could be *any* secular state that was not in *some* way animated by the *libido dominandi*; the sinful desire to dominate animates not only the powers-that-be but also the powers-that-would-be. While discriminate and as such highly fallible political judgments are required of Christians in such contests for power, it is academic child's play not to reckon with these realities, known by reason from historical experience[35] if not by faith from revelation. By the same token, Paul's God institutes and thus employs also empire as a structure for rough justice that militates against the kind of nationalistic zealotries that tormented Palestine in the first century and, likewise, the Europe of the twentieth century in the guises of fascism and Nazism, and, painful truth be told, some forms of Zionism today. Empire, by contrast with fascism, can represent a multicultural cosmopolitanism that forces diverse peoples to live together in a tolerable peace. That empire *forces* peoples to do so

---

behind imperial oppression are exposed and defeated. This *skandalon* brings about a division of the division, retooling the biblical legacy and its categories as well.

32. N. T. Wright, "Paul and Caesar: A New Reading of Romans," in *A Royal Priesthood? The Use of the Bible Ethically and Politically*, ed. Craig Bartholomew et al. (Carlisle: Paternoster, 2002) 173–93.

33. John M. G. Barclay, *Pauline Churches and Diaspora Jews* (Tübingen: Mohr Siebeck, 2011) criticizes Wright's "reading between the lines" to discover a "hidden transcript" (379).

34. Ibid., 386.

35. Michael Burleigh, *Earthly Powers: The Clash of Religion and Politics in Europe from the French Revolution to the Great War* (New York: HarperCollins, 2005).

as a monopoly on the means of coercion is, to be sure, its fatal flaw as but another form of political sovereignty. That is why, theologically, the state is but a temporary order and one that is eminently reformable. Whatever its historical failures, however, empire's best aspiration for cosmopolitan tolerance is not simplistically to be demonized, especially when the political alternative, as we saw in the twentieth century, is the bottomless pit of ethnic-group self-determination over against other ethnicities.[36]

Thus the Paul who also authored Romans 13, according to Barclay, "reads political history according to a different script" such that "his stance towards the Roman Empire is neither simple opposition or obedience: it is a field of human reality criss-crossed and contested (like all others) by the opposing forces of Flesh and Spirit, and is subject to powers far greater than itself in the battle created by the gospel."[37] In this way, Paul "more radically reframes reality"; he demythologizes political sovereignties and reduces them to a "bit-players in a drama scripted by the cross and resurrection of Jesus." This does not mean, according to Barclay, that Paul's gospel is "apolitical, only that the political is for him enmeshed in an all-encompassing power-struggle which covers every domain of life," that is, neither separating the personal from the public nor reducing politics to the contest for the reins of power. Accordingly, "his theology concerns *the subversive and redemptive power of divine grace in Christ, which creates and empowers new communities of social (and therefore broadly political) significance.*"[38] As we have urged in our thesis, then, what we pastors and theologians are to do today, precisely as cutting edge political praxis, is to create and sustain engaged and caring communities of Christ's people as the knowing and articulate alternative to politics as usual, based on the customary separations of the private and the public.[39] Just this, as I shall now note in conclusion,

---

36. See Peter J. Leithart, *Defending Constantine: The Twilight of an Empire and the Dawn of Christendom* (Downers Grove, IL: IVP Academic, 2010). Leithart's "defense" is rather more nuanced than the (intentionally) provocative title indicates. What is troubling, however, even in Leithart is the habitual lack of Western historical awareness that locates Constantine, rather than Charlemagne, as the source of our Euro-American problems. See David Levering Lewis, *God's Crucible: Islam and the Making of Europe, 570–1215* (New York: Norton, 2008). Greater awareness of Western particularity in this regard, incidentally, might provoke Western theology to a thorough-going reconsideration of the filioque controversy; see Richard S. Haugh, *Photius and the Carolingians: The Trinitarian Controversy* (Belmont, MA: Nordland, 1975).

37. Barclay, *Pauline Churches and Diaspora Jews*, 386.

38. Ibid., 383, emphasis added.

39. The dualism of public and private that arises with Cartestian-Kantian subjectivity

opens up a freed place in the world for the formation within the nations of new vocations, including the political vocation, of the baptized.

Ways Forward in the Christian Theology of the Powers

Still the question cannot go begging: if the powers and principalities are not reducible to political sovereignties, even if they manifest in this way by deviation from God's institution and purpose, what in the world are we talking about? The mysteriousness of evil makes it a matter of discernment. Reference to fallen angels or elements of creation claiming the power and principle of origin but gone astray by asserting autonomy over against their Creator, do not much illuminate the question; they merely state it in mythological form. What concerns us is the mystery of genuine evil, that is, of knowing, willful, personal rebellion against the Lord and Giver of life. That conundrum remains unclarified in the biblical depictions. I suggest, then, by way of conclusion the following principles drawn from the foregoing that may help in our deliberation.

First, following a suggestion of Gregory of Nyssa in his *Great Catechism*, might we not be helped today by thinking of the mystery of evil under the concept of *envy*?[40] You may recall Augustine's more familiar (to us in the West) account: he spoke of Lucifer's rage upon learning that the lowly earthlings were elected as God's covenant partner and so resolved to destroy the creation and the covenant. Just so he seduced humanity with the false promise, *sicut Deus eritis*, that tickled their pride. Thus Augustine predominantly discusses this sin under the concept of *superbia*, pride. But notice that the false promise, "You shall be as God," is not premised on a false estimate of human power. It is precisely because they *lack* power, and know they lack it, that they are willing to eat the forbidden fruit that bestows it. Rather, the devil tempts them with his own sin, envy; he captures their desire with envy. The sin of pride that violates the First Table thus forms a circle with the sin of envy at the conclusion of the Second Table. Of course, Augustine knew this as well. Disordered love, *concupiscentia*, dominates the sinner who in pride, as the latter-day Augustinian Martin

---

is what most contemporary theologians think of under the term "the doctrine of the two kingdoms," as if this supposedly represented Luther's political theology. I disentangle this confusion in *Luther and the Beloved Community*, 301–57, and *Before Auschwitz*, 183–87.

40. *Great Catechism* 6 (NPNF[2] 5:481).

Luther put it, "wants to be God and does not want God to be God."[41] Envy, as I argue in my systematic theology,[42] is ontologically prior to greed; greed is but the envy of the rich. As it seems to me, envy is the malice on which the contemporary world turns.

With either accent, however, our bondage to the tyrannical powers at work in human concretions of power but not reducible to them is not innocent victimhood but *sinful*. This easily misunderstood claim is meant in the precise sense of the *ordo caritatis*, where sin refers to the person's relation to God (*coram Deo*), not, then, to its relation to other creatures in political life (*coram humanibus, coram mundo*) where there are indeed significant degrees of guilt or criminality and equally significant differences between victims and perpetrators. But envy is the sin that seduces us to the powers (think, illustratively, of the Bernie Madoff Ponzi scheme: while he sinfully abused his victims they just as sinfully, though not criminally, became his victims in their own greed for a disproportionate financial bonanza). Envy and greed are sinful in the way that yielding to a seduction captivates the heart of human desire that rests truly only in the God of love; and this sinfulness that becomes second nature in fallen humanity in turn requires the patient pastoral work of the ecclesia for its repentance, forgiveness, cleansing, healing and re-ordering in those who are now slowly learning to have in them the same mind that was in Christ Jesus (Phil 2:5–6), who did not envy His divine status but rather gave Himself for lesser and morally unworthy beings.

Second, then, against the tendency in Wink and Wright (let alone lesser imitators) to underplay the reconciliation of the holy God with the sinful creature in the thrall of pride and envy in favor of the liberation of the innocent creature from political tyranny, we might better hold these New Testament atonement motifs, along with the call to cross-bearing discipleship in imitation of the Lord who thus shows us His way, tightly together. As it is stated in the Apocalypse: "Now have come the salvation and the power and the kingdom of our God and the authority of his Messiah, for the accuser of our comrades has been thrown down, who accuses them night and day before our God. But they have conquered him by the blood of the Lamb and by the word of their testimony, for they did not cling to life even in the face of death" (Rev 12:10–11). Here we see an indication of the

---

41. *LW* 31:10.

42. Paul R. Hinlicky, *Beloved Community: Critical Dogmatics after Christendom* (Grand Rapids: Eerdmans, 2015).

unity of all three atonement motifs found in the New Testament: liberation from the tyrannical powers, forgiveness of sin, and freedom to follow Jesus through the cross to the crown.

Commentator Joe Mangina insightfully remarks, "The devil is the original bearer of false witness. His lies are legion, like his multiple personalities. At the social level, they include all the stratagems of deception and doublespeak by which corporations, governments, and the vast enterprises of technocracy seek to keep people from a knowledge of the truth."[43] The devil's lie, that is, his moral fault (I am now adding to Mangina's commentary by way of amplification) is not that we are sinners. That we are sinners is the truth. The lie is that we have not been victoriously befriended. Luther helps here:

> There was no counsel, no help, no comfort for us until this only and eternal Son of God, in his unfathomable goodness, had mercy on us because of our misery and distress and came from heaven to help us. Those tyrants and jailers have not been routed, and their place has been taken by Jesus Christ, the Lord of life, righteousness, and every good and blessing. He has snatched us poor lost creatures from the jaws of hell, won us, made us free, and restored us to the Father's favor and grace. As his own possession he has taken us under his protection and shelter, in order that he may rule us by his righteousness, wisdom, power, life and blessedness.[44]

Note how all three atonement motifs combine here. By winning our forgiveness before God at the cross, Christ dethrones the evil powers whose only real power is the half-truth they possess in accusing sinners, making them unworthy of God and so submissive to their tyranny. But making us worthy of God by His action of generosity, Christ gives His own Spirit to free believers from the threats of death temporal and eternal. The ultimate sanction of the tyrannical powers, the power of Death, is thus contested in the holy battle of the faith of public witnesses, the martyrs.

Third, if political sovereignty is not as such the enemy of God, but is, as Paul affirms in Romans 13, instituted to be God's servant for our good, and as such, is a place of conscientious obedience to God (Rom 13:5), by the same token, the state is all the same, as the same text indicates (Rom 13:4), nothing but an ambiguous monopoly on the means of violence (1

---

43. Joseph L. Mangina, *Revelation* (Grand Rapids: Brazos, 2010) 154.

44. Luther, Large Catechism, in *The Book of Concord*, ed. Robert Kolb and Timothy J. Wengert (Minneapolis: Fortress, 2000) 434.

Sam 8:4–22) by which at best some sinners deter fellow sinners from spiraling one and all downward into anarchic violence. If that is right, Agamben is right, contra Hobbes, to describe political sovereignty, not as the social contract on which civilization is built but as an abiding emergency order that lawlessly enforces law in the time between humanity's fall and its redemption. Likewise, then, Marx was not wrong to imagine that in the coming of the Beloved Community, the state, like the temple, will wither away. In the interim, however, the nations to which the gospel is addressed in the Spirit's mission find themselves under political sovereignty of many kinds that may, or may not, serve according to God's institution. If the ministry of pastors and theologians is *to* the Word and sacraments that they be faithfully and aptly spoken, making in the world a zone of freedom for such discernment, the ministry of all the baptized is *from* the Word and sacraments to the suffering world in need and under thralldom.

Engaging the powers does not happen by preachers abusing the pulpit to indulge in the partisan bromides and bombast of politics as usual, but in the very serious business of empowering the laity for political vocations.[45] Amos Wilder, for pertinent precedence, lifted up in 1964 the great work of the postwar Evangelical Academies in Germany bringing together "jurists, philosophers and sociologists as well as theologians" in *die Zone der Freiheit*, that is, as the ecclesia, to brainstorm the problems of public life in the task of postwar reconstruction.[46] That kind of engagement of the "whole church," as Wilder put it, will be, I submit, the theological method that empowers us to see and to say what in the world we are talking about when we take up, not only Paul's words, but his program of holy struggle "against the principalities, against the powers, against the world rulers of this present darkness, against the spiritual hosts of wickedness in the heavenly places."

---

45. Robert Benne, *The Paradoxical Vision: A Public Theology for the Twenty-First Century* (Minneapolis: Fortress, 1995).

46. Wilder, "Kerygma, Eschatology and Social Ethics," 510.

2

The Powers and Paul's Letter to the Romans

Beverly Roberts Gaventa

ON JULY 27, 1942, Michel Epstein, a Russian émigré of Jewish descent living in occupied France, wrote to the German ambassador, Otto Abetz, on behalf of his wife. Epstein's wife, the novelist Irène Némirovsky, also a Russian émigré of Jewish birth, had lived in France since the 1920s. But on July 13, 1942, she was arrested. Epstein's letter pleads with the ambassador to intervene on behalf of Némirovsky in order to secure her release. First, he attempts to show that Némirovsky is harmless by quoting a letter the two of them had received from the German soldiers who had occupied their town, expressing their thanks for kind treatment. He then explains that his wife is a famous novelist, that she has no interest in politics, that she is a Catholic who, despite her family of origin, has no affection for Jews. Finally he writes, "For many years my wife has been suffering from chronic asthma . . . and internment in a concentration camp would be fatal for her." The letter concludes with an appeal to the ambassador's sense of justice.[1]

---

1. This and other letters related to Némirovsky are published as an appendix to her novel *Suite Française* (New York: Vintage, 2007), recovered and published decades after her death. The letter cited here appears on pp. 403-4.

These words are stunningly naïve to us, reading them nearly three-quarters of a century later. In this and other letters, Epstein displays an awareness that his wife is in danger, but that awareness is accompanied by the expectation that something can be done to rescue her. His letter to the ambassador assumes that the recipient is a rational, moral agent, an agent who values human life—especially the life of a gentle, prominent figure who poses no threat to the German cause. It also assumes that the ambassador will not wish to harm such a person. Epstein inhabits a moral universe in which people without power make requests of those with power, and those requests are (or at least they may be) heard and responded to reasonably.[2]

In 1940, two years before this letter was written, Simone Weil published an extended essay entitled "The *Iliad*, or, The Poem of Force."[3] Although her essay never mentions any contemporary person or event—not Hitler, not Germany, not the French occupation—it is obvious on every line that she is speaking simultaneously of the past and the present.[4] Her reflections on the nature of "force" or power are stirring, both for their unrelenting presentation and for the depth of their insight. She defines force as "that x that turns anybody who is subjected to it into a *thing*."[5] Yet on Weil's reading, the implications of the use of force (power) are not unilateral. She contends that the *Iliad* reveals the devastating, corrosive nature

---

2. It could be objected, to be sure, that Epstein is aware of his audience and may couch his argument in this way simply in order to secure a positive response. His other letters, however, reinforce my observations about his moral universe. At a slightly later point, for example, he suggests that he might be able to exchange places with his wife, in order to rescue her (411–12), and he seeks to send her food, money, and clothing (411). By the time those letters were written, Némirovsky had already been sent to Auschwitz, where she died on August 17, 1942.

3. The original, "L'Iliade ou le poème de la force," was published in *Cahiers du Sud*, December 1940/January 1941. It was later translated by Mary McCarthy and published in English as "The *Iliad*, or, The Poem of Force" (Wallingford, PA: Pendle Hill, 1956). I am grateful to my colleague Jonathan Tran for introducing me to this remarkable essay.

4. Joseph H. Summers characterizes Weil's essay as less a work "about" the *Iliad* than "an extraordinary response to the war with Hitler and the fall of France" ("Notes on Simone Weil's *Iliad*," in *Simone Weil: Interpretations of a Life*, ed. George Abbott White [Amherst: University of Massachusetts Press, 1981] 87). That is not to say that Weil's interest in the *Iliad* was a transient or superficial matter. Adrian Poole reports that when she was to be arrested in 1941, she carried with her only clothing and her copy of the *Iliad* ("Simone Weil: Force, Tragedy, and Grace in Homer's *Iliad*," in *Christian Theology and Tragedy: Theologians, Tragic Literature and Tragic Theory*, ed. Kevin Taylor and Giles Waller [Farnham, UK: Ashgate, 2011] 121).

5. "The *Iliad*," 3.

of force (or power) both for the one who exerts it and for the one who is subjected to it. She also discusses a second sense of equity at work in the *Iliad*, in that it treats the Achaeans and the Trojans so evenhandedly that it is impossible to know on which side the author's sympathies lie.[6] In Weil's moral universe, there is little hope for power that does not corrupt, little expectation of human progress. Despite the fact that Michel Epstein and Simone Weil write from the same country at roughly the same time, they occupy two strikingly different moral universes.

In this essay, I want to put these two texts in conversation with biblical understandings of the "principalities and powers." More specifically, I am concerned with Paul's understanding of anti-god powers as reflected in his letter to the Romans, although along the way I make brief reference to the appearance of the phrase in Colossians and Ephesians.

Disputes among New Testament scholars about the nature and work of the "principalities and powers" are long-standing. In the middle of the last century, Bultmann's demythologizing program set the terms of the debate to which others reacted.[7] Since then, at least in the English-speaking world, the best-known works on the principalities and powers in the New Testament are those of Wesley Carr and Walter Wink.[8] The questions are multiple and complex, having to do with the origin and ontology of the principalities and powers as well as their referents. My own conviction is that New Testament writings assume that the principalities and powers are "real," even if they do not provide us with a systematic account of their origin or status. They are not merely code language for the empire and its agents. Nor are they simply to be internalized in social or psychological terms. To be sure, we may well see or suspect the activity of the principalities and powers in human empires or within ourselves, but they cannot be reduced to such.

---

6. Michael Ferber, who otherwise identifies some important shortcomings in Weil's analysis of the *Iliad*, agrees that the poem is pervaded by a "tone of impartiality" ("Simone Weil's *Iliad*," in *Simone Weil: Interpretations of a Life*, 63–85 [quotation on 76]).

7. Bultmann's program is not focused exclusively or even primarily on the "principalities and powers," although they are clearly implicated; see his "New Testament and Mythology," in vol. 1 of *Kerygma and Myth: A Theological Debate*, ed. Hans Werner Bartsch, trans. Reginald H. Fuller (London: SPCK, 1953) 1–44. This essay originally appeared in 1941 in *Offenbarung und Heilsgeschehen* (Munich: A. Lempp).

8. Wesley Carr, *Angels and Principalities: The Background, Meaning, and Development of the Pauline Phrase "hai archai kai hai exousiai,"* SNTSMS 42 (Cambridge: Cambridge University Press, 1981); Walter Wink, *Naming the Powers: The Language of Power in the New Testament* (Philadelphia: Fortress, 1984).

Epstein and Romans

Returning now to Michel Epstein we see, or so I suggest, that in the moral universe of Epstein's letter, there are choices to make. The letter assumes that having a full account of Némirovsky's life and importance and relationships will—or at least it could—prompt the ambassador to do the right thing. Because the ambassador is a just person (Paul would say a *dikaios* person, an upright or righteous person), Epstein imagines that he will elect to do the right thing.[9] He has a choice to make, and armed with the right information, he could make that choice. It is a matter of educating him, of moving him. Implicit in the letter's rhetoric is a plea that the ambassador act as the just person he is, that he not side with injustice, with wrongdoing. With no great leap of the imagination, and by selecting our texts carefully, we can read Paul's letter to the Romans in just this way. As he develops his accusation about the universal extent of human sinfulness in the early part of the letter, Paul observes that those who do what is right will be rewarded, while those who do the wrong will be punished. Repeated statements about faith and salvation are consistent with the view that the gospel is an offer made by God in Jesus Christ, that people make a response to that new possibility, and then they stand on one side or the other of a line (10:13 and elsewhere). When in 8:13 Paul writes that those who live by the flesh will die and those who live by the Spirit are God's sons and daughters, he reinforces this view. It is found abundantly in commentaries and other interpretations of Romans.

When we read Epstein's letter with this notion of human choice, however, we run into a problem. We already know that his position (whether it is genuine optimism or a desperate rhetorical strategy) is deeply flawed.[10] We know (or at least we strongly and rightly suspect) that the ambassador will not intervene. Indeed, the ambassador cannot intervene; in fact, it is already too late, as Némirovsky is on her way to Auschwitz even as her

---

9. Interestingly, Matthew's Gospel describes Joseph as a "righteous" person when he contemplates ending his engagement to Mary because of her pregnancy; that is, this "righteous" act Joseph anticipates has the potential to destroy the life of Mary and, by implication, that of her unborn baby. See the discussion in Gaventa, *Mary: Glimpses of the Mother of Jesus* (Columbia: University of South Carolina Press, 1995) 40–42.

10. In her preface to the French edition of *Suite Française*, Myriam Anissimov contends that Epstein did not understand the seriousness of the situation and adds, "Every day he expected her to come home and insisted, at mealtimes, that her place be set at the table" (428).

husband pleads for assistance.[11] And perhaps most achingly, although we may well identify with Epstein's vulnerability, his terror, his urgent desire to pull any lever that may be helpful, we see that he is himself already reinscribing the very hatred against which he is fighting: she has no affection for Jews, he insists, thereby siding with the powerful in a futile attempt to win favor for his own disempowered wife.

Simone Weil and Romans

Recognizing that the naïve optimism on the surface of Epstein's letter is undermined not only by concrete historical circumstances but by the letter itself, we return to Romans, where we find that the notion of good and evil, of the righteous and the unrighteous, is significantly more complicated than my earlier highly selective reading suggests. Paul does not simply write that outside of the intervention of God in the death and resurrection of Jesus Christ everyone does what is wrong, that everyone sins, that no one does the good. He also contends that this happens *because* there are agents in the world by the names of Sin and Death, and these agents have humanity—all of humanity—under their control.[12] To be sure, human disobedience opens the door for the agents (humans are not merely passive objects), but once Sin and Death are unleashed, their power is both universal and unavoidable. I think this understanding is implicit already in Romans 1, but it comes into full view in chapters 5–6. Adam's disobedience brought Sin and Death into the world, where they established themselves as enslaving rulers.

It is precisely at this point that I find Simone Weil's essay on the *Iliad* so instructive, as her comments about force (or power) help us unpack Paul's language and understand that it is no mere rhetorical flourish. Weil writes about the destructive character of force: force has "the ability to turn a human being into a thing while he is still alive. He is alive; he has a soul; and

---

11. She died on August 17, 1942, and Epstein himself was arrested in October of that same year and died in Auschwitz on November 6 (ibid., 428–29).

12. For elaboration on this point, see Gaventa, "The Cosmic Power of Sin in Paul's Letter to the Romans," in *Our Mother Saint Paul* (Louisville: Westminster John Knox, 2007) 125–36; Gaventa, "God Handed Them Over," in ibid., 113–23; Gaventa, "The Rhetoric of Violence and the God of Peace in Paul's Letter to the Romans," in *Paul, John, and Apocalyptic Eschatology: Studies in Honour of Martinus C. de Boer*, ed. Jan Krans et al., NovTSup 149 (Leiden: Brill, 2013) 61–75.

yet—he is a thing."[13] Life in such a state is "life that death congeals before abolishing."[14] Force enslaves.[15] "Regularly, every morning, the soul castrates itself of aspiration, for thought cannot journey through time without meeting death on the way.... The mind ought to find a way out, but the mind has lost all capacity to so much as look outward. The mind is completely absorbed in doing itself violence."[16]

Here we have an eloquent companion to Paul's comments about the twinned relationship between the powers (the powerful force, in Weil's language) of Sin and Death. When Sin enters the world through Adam, Sin unleashes Death itself, not simply Death as human finitude but Death in the midst of human life. In the second half of Romans 6, Paul claims that human beings were nothing more than the weapons of Sin, although the word "weapons" is often rendered by the vague term, "instruments." Human beings were Sin's slaves, that is, identified only as the obedient property of Sin and Death (6:12–23). Chapter 7 takes the argument further still: even those who knew the good and right and holy Law of God were unable to follow that Law, reduced as they were to a Death-defined existence (7:24).

As noted earlier, Simone Weil realizes that the use of force is not only death-dealing for the one on the receiving end. It destroys both the powerful and the disempowered. "Force is as pitiless to the man who possesses it, or thinks he does, as to its victims; the second it crushes, the first it intoxicates. The truth is, nobody really possesses it."[17] Paul does not reflect on this question in quite the same way, but there is a suggestion of this mutual destruction in his citation of Psalm 139:4 in Romans 3:13: "The venom of asps is under their tongues." Human speech is so toxic that it poisons both the speaker and the one addressed.[18] Weil understands that the intoxication of power allows those with power (temporary power, for power is always temporary) to persuade themselves that they are different, even that they

---

13. "The *Iliad*," 4–5.
14. Ibid., 8.
15. Ibid., 10.
16. Ibid., 22. In these lines Weil anticipates some of Orlando Patterson's important observations about slavery in his influential study *Slavery and Social Death: A Comparative Study* (Cambridge, MA: Harvard University Press, 1982).
17. "The *Iliad*," 11.
18. See Gaventa, "From Toxic Speech to the Redemption of Doxology in Paul's Letter to the Romans," in *The Word Leaps the Gap: Essays on Scripture and Theology in Honor of Richard B. Hays*, ed. J. Ross Wagner et al. (Grand Rapids: Eerdmans, 2008) 392–408.

belong to a different species from those whom they have disempowered.[19] It is precisely this dividing of the world into the insider and the outsider that Paul resists throughout Romans. There is a difference between Jew and Gentile, yes, but that difference derives solely from God's historic initiative with Israel and it does not license either Jewish boasting about God's favor (3:27–31) or Gentile arrogance in the face of Israel's "disbelief" (11:17–24).

It is possible to dismiss both Paul and Weil as being too pessimistic about human potential.[20] It is also possible to read the first half of Romans and think that Paul's language about the death-dealing consequences of Sin is limited to the "spiritual" (however such a limitation is possible) or even that it is so abstract as to be worthless. Or it might be suggested that Paul exaggerates the human problem in order to intensify the need for the gospel; that is, this is all a rhetorical strategy. These are but a few among the many strategies we have for not hearing what the text actually says. Reading Romans 1–8 alongside Simone Weil's discussion of the *Iliad* in the shadow of the Third Reich disrupts that fantasy, or at least that is my hope.[21]

My purpose is to extend both Paul's analysis of Sin and Weil's of power into our contemporary context. Consider the phenomenon of the child soldier. Torn from his home, he is forced into a life of hatred and violence, a life that gradually becomes his own worldview as well. Or consider the girl bartered by impoverished families or grabbed off the street of her city, again forced into prostitution under threat of violence and even death. Few readers of North American theological journals will have first-hand experience of these widespread phenomena in our own world, but we do at least occasionally glimpse our collective enslavement to a view of the world (politically, economically, environmentally) that has us smiling all the while we are destroying our own planet, to say nothing of our children's future.

A thought experiment will be helpful. Imagine sending a slight revision of Michel Epstein's letter on behalf of a thirteen-year-old ripped from his home and compelled to fight in someone else's war. Shall we imagine that this child will be liberated because we ask? Shall we imagine that

19. "The *Iliad*," 13.

20. In his essay "Simon Weil's *Iliad*," Michael Ferber does not quite dismiss Weil, but he does struggle to get past what he sees as her pessimism and disillusion about human nature.

21. Weil's concerns about the relentlessness of power are captured movingly in the recent adaptation of the *Iliad* by Lisa Peterson and Denis O'Hare (originally produced by the New York Theatre Workshop, 2012; script available from Dramatists Play Service, 2013).

his captors are themselves free agents who can release him? The cycle of Sin that produces Death that produces Sin is not to be broken by human resolve. It is all too easy for Western Christians to appeal to free will or conscience, because we live in a world of options (or at least we imagine we have options). Simone Weil helps us glimpse the extent of Paul's insights.

The Powers in Romans 8

As longtime readers of Paul we know that this universal human enslavement to the powers of Sin and Death is not where his letter ends. He first argues (in 5:12–21) that the reign of Sin and Death is overcome by Christ's obedience, so that grace reigns even more powerfully than do Sin and Death. Because Death and Sin no longer reign over Christ (6:6–11), they no longer reign over the baptized as well. In the flesh of Jesus Christ, God condemns Sin (8:3) and frees humanity from the reign of Sin and Death. As a result of this liberative action on God's part, Paul writes that "you received a spirit of adoption," becoming God's heirs, even fellow heirs of Christ (8:15–16). If "we" cry out for the fullness of God's redemption, we do so as those who already have the first fruit of the Spirit. The Spirit intercedes for those whom God has chosen, called, and rectified (8:28–30).

This complex argument culminates in the well-known claim at the end of Romans 8 that nothing in all of creation will be able to separate "us" from God's love in and through Jesus Christ our lord. First, Paul lists a number of circumstances of human suffering: hardship, distress, persecution, famine, nakedness, peril, sword (NRSV).

Some of these circumstances presuppose the activity of another human party (at least persecution and the sword); others are more ambiguous. A second list follows in verses 38–39, this time perhaps a list of those agents that produce the circumstances:

- death and life
- angels and rulers
- things present and things to come
- powers
- height and depth
- any other created thing

A few observations are crucial.[22] First, this is a comprehensive list. Even if we cannot precisely identify the referent of "height and depth," for example, we can see that he means everything that is. "Any other created thing" clinches that observation: nothing that is outside of or apart from the Creator can separate humanity from its rightful Lord. The precise phrase, "principalities and powers" does not appear here, but I think it is safe to assume that the notion of "principalities and powers" is included in this comprehensive list. Paul's comments come quite close to those of Ephesians 6:12: "Our struggle is not against enemies of blood and flesh, but against the rulers, against the authorities, against the cosmic powers of this present darkness, against the spiritual forces of evil in the heavenly places" (NRSV).

The comprehensive character of the list also prevents us (or so I would hope) from imagining that the powers are to be identified narrowly with powers of the state, whether that means the Roman Empire or any other. A great deal of scholarly energy has been expended in recent years in arguing that Paul (and other New Testament writers, although my concern at present is with Paul) is anti-empire. And, by drawing on two texts from the French Occupation, it might be assumed that I am identifying the principalities and powers specifically with the modern nation-state in its most extreme form of a consumptive drive for power.[23] Although I agree that the implications of Paul's gospel are at odds with any human reign (once we say "Jesus is Lord," then Caesar is not), I think that Paul's gospel has far larger enemies in view than the puny Roman Empire or any other merely human edifice.[24] These may be evidence of the work of the powers, but they cannot be identified narrowly with the work of the powers.

Although the list is comprehensive of human life, curiously it does not include the power named Sin. Here Death is partnered with Life rather than with Sin. At first glance that seems odd, since Sin and Death have

---

22. For an orientation to the scholarly discussion, see Robert Jewett, *Romans: A Commentary*, ed. Eldon Jay Epp, Hermeneia (Minneapolis: Fortress, 2007) 550–54; Arland J. Hultgren, *Paul's Letter to the Romans: A Commentary* (Grand Rapids: Eerdmans, 2011) 340–42; Wink, *Naming the Powers*, 47–50; Carr, *Angels and Principalities*, 112–14.

23. Perhaps even worse, it may be suspected that I am offering the Apostle Paul as the "answer" to the Holocaust. Here I am reminded of David Weiss Halvini's plea that no answer should be attempted, as "merely asking the question" implies "that there is an answer, a just answer" (*The Book and the Sword: A Life of Learning in the Shadow of Destruction* [New York: Farrar, Straus and Giroux, 1996] 154).

24. See especially John M. G. Barclay, "Why the Roman Empire was Insignificant to Paul," in *Pauline Churches and Diaspora Jews*, WUNT 1.275 (Tübingen: Mohr Siebeck, 2011) 362–87.

played such a prominent role in chapters 5–7. Paul suppresses reference to Sin here (i.e., Sin as a power, uppercase Sin), perhaps because he has already declared it to be vanquished by God in the death of Jesus Christ (8:3), and he has insisted that "we" are no longer Sin's slaves. The powers on the list are nonetheless intertwined with sinning in that they produce it. Sin is suppressed in this list but certainly not erased from a humanity that lives under its threat.

And the word *threat* is necessary. Even if we cannot say precisely who these powers are ontologically or historically, it is clear that Paul understands them to be "real" and that they pose a continuing threat. The whole shape and tenor of this passage requires that reading. From the moment he asks the question of 8:31, "If God is acting on our behalf, then who can be against us?" Paul is engaging in what we would call trash talk. He is calling out God's own enemies: "Who can bring an accusation against God's own chosen? Who can condemn? Finally, who can separate?" In more contemporary language, what Paul says is, "Bring it on!"

Whatever we can and cannot say about these powers historically and ontologically, it seems clear that Paul thinks there *are* powers and that they have acted and are acting and will continue to act to separate humanity from God. (And that point seems reinforced by 1 Corinthians 15, by Philippians 2:5–11, as well as by the other "principalities and powers" passages.) The struggle continues, but victory is assured. "We" are, Paul writes, more than conquerors. So, as we consider the work of the powers in our own time, we join our voices to the chorus stretching back across time to declare that God will have the last word, that God will triumph. As Paul writes in 16:20, "The God of peace will soon crush Satan under your feet."

The Church and the Powers

It is tempting, then, to think that "we"—the church, the community of the baptized—"we" are separate from the powers. And Ephesians encourages us to do just that, with its comment that "we" contend with the powers (6:12). Colossians also claims that they have been "disarmed" (2:15). With the encouragement of such assertions, "we" are able to construe ourselves as the rectified children of God who are under attack by powers that are "over there" or "out there," powers that are other than us and in opposition to us. And I hear Christian talk that moves in that direction. I do not mean simply that there are right-wing, triumphalist Christians who isolate themselves in sectarian fashion over against the rest of the world. I have in mind also those who, justifiably anxious about the church's present and future, would seek to reinforce the church's boundaries against an increasingly disturbing world. A reading of Romans 8 that makes a sharp distinction between the church and the world, or at least between the church and the principalities and powers, can be very attractive.

I want to trouble that conclusion a bit by reading further in the letter. Admittedly, Paul does not use the language of powers later in the letter. The remainder of the letter nonetheless demonstrates that the "we"—the rectified, justified, glorified—"we" are nonetheless at risk.

Immediately after this moving declaration at the end of chapter 8 that nothing will separate "us," Paul takes up the question of God's dealings with Israel. That way of formulating the description is important: Romans 9–11 is not primarily concerned with Jewish unbelief or Jewish disobedience. Romans 9–11 is primarily concerned with God. It begins with doxology (9:5) and it ends with doxology (11:33–36). Paul's concern is to show that, however things may appear at present, God is the creator and sustainer of Israel. God's commitment to Israel is unbreakable (11:29). The argumentative edge of 9–11 is not directed against Jewish unbelief or Jewish disobedience, but against Gentile arrogance and condescension.[25]

In 11:13, Paul steps outside of his account of God's division of Israel into two parts, the remnant and the remainder. He writes, "Now I am talking to you Gentiles." What follows is a sharp warning about the danger of condescension to others, particularly to those Jews who are part of the "remainder" of Israel, those who do not confess Jesus as Lord. "Do not boast," he writes in verse 18. To paraphrase only slightly, "God grafted you into the tree, and God can take you out again." It is all too easy for Christians to read this passage and assume that the condescension Paul addresses has to do only with a group of first century Gentiles who thought too highly of themselves because of their belief in Jesus, but I think his warning is not to be restricted to the first century. Anytime we understand our faith as our possession, our achievement, our prerogative—a prerogative that sets us

---

25. Space does not permit a defense of this reading, but see Gaventa, "On the Calling-into-Being of Israel: Rom 9:6–29," in *Between Gospel and Election: Explorations in the Interpretation of Romans 9–11*, ed. Florian Wilk and J. Ross Wagner, WUNT 257 (Tübingen: Mohr Siebeck, 2010) 255–69; Gaventa, "Questions about *Nomos*, Answers about *Christos*: Romans 10:4 in Context," in *Torah Ethics and Early Christian Identity*, edited by Susan J. Wendel and David M. Miller (Grand Rapids: Eerdmans, 2016), 121–34.

apart from others so as to make them inferior—then we become the objects of Paul's admonition.

That warning about condescension recurs, although for other reasons, in Romans 14 where Paul discusses conflicts over shared meals. To oversimplify what is anything but simple in the text, not to mention the secondary literature, the situation is as follows: some Roman Christians (Jews as well as Gentiles) believed that they were no longer bound by Jewish dietary laws and could eat whatever they wanted (the "garbage bellies"); other Roman Christians (Gentiles as well as Jews) believed that Jewish dietary laws were continually in force and therefore ate only vegetables (the "lettuce eaters"). This dispute not only makes it difficult to plan the church's potluck supper; it threatens the community's wholeness. Paul's response is, first, to recall for both sides the fact that Jesus is Lord, and they are not. There is to be no judgment of the other, since the other belongs to Jesus Christ.

But he does not stop there—with mere tolerance. He goes on to concede that he himself sides with the "garbage bellies." "Nothing is inherently unclean," he writes in 14:14, going even further in verse 17, "The kingdom of God is not food and drink." Although he agrees with the "garbage bellies," that endorsement does not permit them to do as they please. They must act so as not to destroy their fellow believers. The "strength" available to them dare not become power to harm the other, power to corrupt the other.

In his Romans commentary, Karl Barth describes Romans 14 as addressed to those who have read and rightly understood the letter. Barth goes on to identify the "garbage bellies," those usually identified as "the strong" (although not by Paul), with the liberals of his own day. This is an idiosyncratic interpretation, and it completely ignores a raft of historical questions. Yet I think that, as so often, Barth has taken us into the heart of this passage. It is those who *do* understand, who are grasped by the gospel's radical grace, who *do* catch a glimpse of the universal implications of the gospel—they are the very ones who are most at risk for behavior that is destructive of others. That is the case because they, in Barth's words, make of their "freedom a concrete thing" and thereby make themselves "weaker than the weak."[26]

Again: Paul does not use the language of principalities and powers in this discussion. But even without the terminology, in Romans 9–11 and

---

26. *The Epistle to the Romans*, trans. Edwyn C. Hoskyns (London: Oxford University Press, 1933) 509.

again in 14, his argument reflects the awareness that Christians continue to be vulnerable to the grasp of the powers. That is why, however positive the triumphal note at the end of Romans 8 may be, it nonetheless presupposes that Christians—along with the rest of creation—live in a combat zone. Creation exists in the battlefield in which the major combatants are God and the anti-God powers. And our role as weapons (the language Paul uses in 6:13) depends on God's action, not our own.

What Does God's Power Look Like?

Paul's claim that the defeat of the powers comes about solely by powerful divine intervention is crucial. At numerous points, his letters give expression to this conviction: Romans 16:20 promises that "the God of peace will quickly crush Satan under your feet." According to Galatians 1:4, Jesus Christ gave himself "that he might deliver us from the present evil age." First Corinthians 15 depicts Christ's resurrection as God's powerful confrontation with death (Death?), the first stage in God's triumph over all enemies (15:25–27). The Philippians hymn culminates with the submission of all creation to the "name of Jesus." As noted above, Colossians 2:15 regards the powers as already disarmed.

In these and other ways, then, we see the conviction that it is God—God alone—who defeats the principalities and powers of this world. That may seem to be a call to Christian passivity in the face of the many evils in our world, so let me emphatically deny any such conclusion. After all, Paul does also admonish the Roman congregations to present themselves as "weapons" of God's righteousness, and of course Ephesians admonishes the putting on of God's armor. But understanding that God is the major power in this conflict is crucial, since otherwise we identify our own projects with those of God without understanding that we are just as vulnerable to being wrong as are all other children of Adam and Eve.[27] Alongside the call for us to be "weapons" of righteousness, we must also always hear the warnings against thinking too highly of ourselves.

Yet this emphasis on divine power seems to reinscribe the difficulties of power, perhaps simply projecting our own wish for power onto

---

27. Renewed evidence for this assertion, if any such is needed, will be found in Charles Marsh's recent biography of Dietrich Bonhoeffer, particularly in the recounting of the capitulation of German Christianity to Nazi propaganda (*Strange Glory: A Life of Dietrich Bonhoeffer* [New York: Knopf, 2014]).

God. Simone Weil's argument about the danger of power for the one who wields it comes to mind here, along with other contemporary theological voices. First, it is necessary to insist that, for Paul at least, God's power is not malevolent. Far from it: God's power is the power to redeem. Recall that, on Weil's definition, power (force) "is that *x* that turns anybody who is subjected to it into a *thing*."[28] Paul would, I submit, recognize this as an apt description of the principalities and powers of this world, particularly Sin and Death, but he would insist that God's power works in exactly the opposite fashion. It is that which turns the things we have become into new creations, creations able to glorify and praise God and to upbuild one another and the entirety of the human community.

God's power, then, is not a larger, more awesome version of human power. After all, the Pauline account of God's power in Jesus Christ does not begin with the resurrection but with the cross. It looks not simply like weakness but like foolishness. It is the power of the divine taking on flesh to redeem us, not just from ourselves, but from all that holds us hostage. It is, in the words of the ending of Romans, "the God of peace who will crush Satan" (16:20). That is to say, it is God who wages peace on behalf of us all.

---

28. "The *Iliad*," 3.

3

Does It Matter That Constantine Ended Sacrifice and Was Baptized?

Vigen Guroian

ON MAY 21ST OF each year, the Orthodox Church commemorates the blessed memories of Saints Constantine the Great and his mother, Helena. The Byzantine Liturgy declares them both "equal to the apostles." The thematic hymn for the feast of Saint Constantine reads as follows:

> Having seen the figure of the Cross in the heavens,
> And like Paul not having received his call from men, O Lord,
> Thy apostle among rulers, the Emperor Constantine,
> Was set by thy hand as ruler over the Imperial City
> That he preserved in peace for many years,
> Through the prayers of the Theotokos, O Only Lover of Mankind.

Now to the minds of many Western Christians, this memorial for the first Christian emperor seems misplaced, if not downright wrongheaded. Never mind the deaths of several family members, including a wife and son, for which there is some reason to suspect Constantine was responsible; over the centuries, there have arisen several interpretations of Constantine's character and career that do not lend themselves to the appellation of saint.

For example, there is the once widely held view that Constantine was a pragmatist or political opportunist who feigned conversion to Christianity in his ambitions for power. Another more generous interpretation is that Constantine, while a religious or superstitious individual, never truly embraced the Christian deity—in other words, that Constantine practiced a religious syncretism suited to the goal of unifying the empire. Even if, in the end, he embraced an overarching monotheism, this might just as easily have been represented by the solar deity to which he paid particular homage in his early years as by the Christian God to whom he offered worship later on.[1]

Then, of course, there is the broader uncomplimentary thesis about Constantine's political and religious legacy. It is that Constantine was the founder of a Christian form of oriental theocracy in which the king stands above the law and the Church is subordinate and servile to the state. This has been called caesaropapism.

Reformed and Protestant thinkers from Luther on have espoused versions of church history in which the original purity of the New Testament church and the apostolic era was corrupted by an unholy alliance of ecclesiastics and secular rulers that radically compromised the gospel; and Constantine, whose life spanned the late third through the mid-fourth century, is remembered as the first to have poisoned the water.

The Radical Reformation spun the narrative of a pacifist church hijacked and turned against Jesus's own nonviolent convictions by the likes of Constantine. In our day, John Howard Yoder adroitly brought this narrative and its underlying thesis up to date. Yoder gave the label "Constantinianism" to this story of church compromise, corruption, and even apostasy.

In his book *Defending Constantine: The Twilight of an Empire and the Dawn of Christendom*, Peter Leithart summarizes the several meanings that Yoder invested in this moniker. Constantinianism is "a wedding of piety to power," a harmful "merger" of church and state in which the movement of God in history is identified with empire, nation, or ruler. Constantinianism also denotes "a set of mental, spiritual, and institutional habits" that deviates from the original gospel of the kingdom of God and the nonviolent teachings of Jesus.[2]

I believe that Leithart is correct that for Yoder "Constantinianism is not [even] dependent upon Constantine." He reminds us that Yoder finds

---

1. See Charles Matson Odahl, *Constantine and the Christian Empire*, 2nd ed. (London: Routledge, 2010) 285.

2. Peter J. Leithart, *Defending Constantine: The Twilight of an Empire and the Dawn of Christendom* (Downers Grove, IL: IVP Academic, 2010) 175, 287, 310.

Constantinianism in the behavior of the Church before Constantine's reign, even in pre-Christian Judaism.[3] While this is true, the fact is that Yoder identifies this misdirection of the Christian mainstream with Constantine in the fourth century.

Does Constantine merit Yoder's pejorative terminology? Leithart believes that he does not, and I agree. In the course of his defense of Constantine and his legacy, Leithart advances the thesis that through a series of actions in which he set himself against pagan sacrifice, Constantine brought an end to Rome as he had known it and opened space for the Christian faith to become the foundation of a new order that we call Christendom. This achievement is, however, not the simple equivalent of Yoder's "Constantinianism." Two of the actions Leithart discusses are, first, Constantine's refusal to offer the customary animal sacrifice after his conquest at the Milvian Bridge in 312, and second, his mandate, through his Edict on Religion of 325, that Roman officials refrain from making animal sacrifices.

Before discussing further this important issue of sacrifice and desacrification of the empire, I must lodge one criticism of *Defending Constantine* that also applies to much of what has been written on Constantine and his relationship to the Church. Leithart neglects to consult Orthodox historians and theologians in his assessment of Constantine's political theology. More broadly, the mind of the Eastern Church is almost entirely absent from *Defending Constantine*, excepting the absolutely obligatory discussion and analysis of Eusebius of Caesarea. But how can one consider Constantine's legacy without at least some discussion of the course of the Byzantine Empire and its worldview?

Several years ago, at a symposium on *Defending Constantine*, I wondered out loud what kind of a book it might have been had Leithart not sparred with John Howard Yoder throughout. For, as it stands, Yoder is the ever-present shadow in the chiaroscuro of Leithart's portrait of Constantine. This, in my view, limits the book, as Leithart never breaks free of the false narratives and misleading historical constructs about Constantine and his legacy that dominate in the academy even today.

Does it matter that Constantine ended sacrifice and was baptized? The Orthodox response is yes, of course. And the hymn I cited at the start gives a strong clue to how Orthodoxy has interpreted Constantine and his legacy such that the answer would be in the affirmative. Among recent Orthodox writers, Alexander Schmemann, John Meyendorff, and

---

3. Ibid., 310.

John McGuckin have assessed Constantine and Byzantium; and their views represent a broad consensus of Orthodox scholarship. They consider the standard Western criticisms, yet, in the final analysis, all work out of an Orthodox memory and ecclesiology. This amounts to a view on the Church's relationship to the world that neither Leithart nor Yoder imagines, or for that matter Gibbon, Burkhart, or Harnack before them.

In his early volume *The Historical Road of Eastern Orthodoxy* (English edition published in 1963), and once again in his later collection of essays *Church, World, Mission*, published in 1979, Alexander Schmemann pauses to interpret the thematic hymn of the Feast of Saints Constantine and Helena. Schmemann finds a special significance in the hymn's proclamation that Constantine, "like Paul," received his call not "from men" but from God and Christ. He maintains that this belief of the Church is crucial in order to understand what made Byzantium tick and what kind of political theology it embraced. "In the eyes of the Eastern tradition," it is critical, he writes, that Christ directly elected and called Constantine, "not even through the Church," "not as an 'individual,' but precisely as emperor." In other words, "the event of that election occurs at a crucial moment of . . . [Constantine's] imperial career, his acceptance of Christ being the condition of his victory over his enemies," namely, Maxentius and his army at the Milvian Bridge in October 312. Thus, in the person of the emperor, Schmemann continues, "the empire acknowledge[d] as its own Kyrios the Lord of heaven and earth, [and] place[d] itself in the perspective and under the dominion of His Kingdom."[4] This is the heart of the Church's confessional narrative, and none of this should be judged as a departure from the Church's biblical and apostolic orientation toward the world or as a tragic compromise with the principalities and powers of this world.

Similarly, in his book *Imperial Unity and Christian Divisions*, John Meyendorff argues that "by allying itself to the Empire, the Church ceased to be a sect accessible to only a few. It assumed 'catholic' responsibility for society as a whole"—and without renouncing "its eschatological calling."[5] In the sixth century, Justinian gave an ideology to this alliance. The Justinian *symphonia*, Meyendorff continues, was never, in its best representation,

---

4. Alexander Schmemann, *Church, World, Mission: Reflections on Orthodoxy in the West* (Crestwood, NY: St. Vladimir's Seminary Press, 1979) 35. See also Schmemann, *The Historical Road of Eastern Orthodoxy*, trans. Lydia W. Kesich (Crestwood, NY: St. Vladimir's Seminary Press, 1977) 62–63.

5. John Meyendorff, *Imperial Unity and Christian Divisions: The Church 450–680 AD* (Crestwood, NY: St. Vladimir's Seminary Press, 1989) 19.

an expectation of a complete transfiguration of the social, economic and political realm, though significantly, at times, it could take on that sort of utopian character. It was, rather, a prescription for bringing about a Christian order and culture in a still fallen world, with a mind that the kingdom of God, while at hand, belongs not to this aeon but to that which is yet coming.

Schmemann maintains that the mistake Western observers often make in their assessments of the Byzantine relationship of Church and empire is to interpret this arrangement as a fundamentally legal or juridical one between "two *institutions,* two *powers,* two *governments.*"[6] To the contrary, he argues, the relationship, which was worked out over centuries and evolved, was premised in a shared faith. This was commenced when Constantine stunned a persecuted Church by granting it freedom in the so-called Edict of Milan of 313 and ultimately his imperial favor. With the background of past persecutions, the Church would interpret these events as providential and the fulfillment of the story of Israel in the Old Testament.

In contrast to the debate in the Latin West, there was not an argument in Byzantium over whether one of these institutions (or regimes), the imperial throne or the Church, is superior to the other. John McGuckin explains: "The biblical doctrine of the 'conditional' blessing from God upon his people for their political stability" comes to play in such a way that the monarchy is bounded and limited by God's covenant with it and by God's law. He argues that this biblical inheritance decisively modified the inherited classical model of absolute sacral kingship.[7] In the end, this was neither caesaropapism nor an assertion of the superiority of the Church over the imperial power.

In an important essay titled "The Legacy of the 13th Apostle," McGuckin reviews the commonly held views that the Byzantine synthesis either persisted to be patently pagan or evolved into caesaropapism. He writes, "The concept of *symphonia* . . . [was] fundamentally faithful to the biblical witness that 'salvation' is first and foremost understood in terms of the gracious restoration and renewal of a people" that overcomes even "numerous

---

6. Schmemann, *Church, World, Mission,* 34.

7. John McGuckin, "The Legacy of the 13th Apostle: Origins of the East Christian Conceptions of Church and State Relation," *St. Vladimir's Theological Review* 47 (2003) 285.

failures" to achieve the "socio-political and moral dimensions of life"[8] to which God calls them.

Further, the Roman understandings of *potestas*, the effective administrative exercise of political and military power, and *auctoritas*, moral authority with the power to judge, were reinterpreted within a new framework under the lordship of Jesus Christ. The horizon of Christ's rule on earth, the eschatological kingdom of God, set parameters of what might be claimed by imperial power or ecclesiastical authority. McGuckin describes "the practical working-out" of the Byzantine *symphonia* as follows:

> In . . . the Byzantine concept of *symphonia*, no one ever denied the emperor's right to command the allegiance of clergy, and their obedience, in all state matters . . . No one in Byzantium (at least no one who ever got far enough from the capital to express the matter freely) ever doubted, equally, that if the emperor strayed too far in matters relating to conscience and orthodoxy (if he transgressed the limits of orthodoxy, that is, which was carefully regulated by the written and synodical tradition) his authority was rendered void, and his throne was endangered by the very fact that he had demonstrated that he no longer had sacral protection as the defender of the true faith.[9]

McGuckin concludes that the Byzantine political theology was dialectical. On the one hand, the state understood that the Church's alliance with it was conditional. God's investment of the emperor with power of sacral dimension placed limits on the autocracy. On the other hand, the Church did not claim any power (i.e., *potestas*) over the imperial rulership. We mustn't forget that this was an age in which our modern distinction between religious and secular political power is not imagined. Even within this Christian universe, political power is invested with sacral meaning. The political authority, however, must respect the "fundamental biblical teaching that the Kingdom of God is not to be identified with the concerns of the powers of this world."[10] The Church only is the sacramental body of Christ that gives access to the kingdom of Heaven.

I have suggested that the genius of Peter Leithart's *Defending Constantine* is a property of his thesis that the revolution Constantine initiated may be traced back to the desacrification of the empire that he initiated. This,

---

8. Ibid.
9. Ibid., 286.
10. Ibid., 287.

says Leithart, is a fact to which the labels of caesaropapism and Constantinianism both are blind. We are reminded again that Constantine commenced his revolution immediately on the heels of his victory over Maxentius at the Milvian Bridge. The practice of all the Emperors that preceded him was to offer a public sacrifice to Jupiter upon entering the city. On that significant occasion, Constantine withheld from doing just that. "Diocletian's empire was built on sacrifice," Leithart explains, but "Constantine," whether he realized it at the time or not, "made it clear that a new theology was coming to be, a political theology without sacrifice."[11] He continues: "By eliminating the civic sacrifice that founded Rome and protecting and promoting the Eucharistic *civitas*, Constantine was, in effect, if not in intent, acknowledging the church's" sole authority in the sacral realm.[12]

No doubt, something profound and revolutionary did indeed happen when Constantine refused to make public sacrifices to the pagan deity. I am in agreement with Leithart's conclusion that "when Constantine began to end sacrifice, he began to end Rome as he knew it."[13] Nonetheless, I do not think Leithart argues his case even as strongly as he might. There was more entailed with Constantine's action than merely the desacrification of the empire: for by refusing the pagan sacrifice, Constantine also laid aside his lawful claim to divinity. And by so doing, he gave to the Church complete and exclusive authority to offer the eucharistic sacrifice instead. Thus—and this alone is ever so significant—Constantine granted the Church the room and permission to freely constitute itself within the empire as the unique "polity" of the kingdom of God.

Again, whether or not he initially intended it, when Constantine refused to perform public sacrifices and conceded that it was not his function to serve the eucharistic sacrifice, he allowed that the Hellenic concept of emperor as absolute ruler over one human and divine Commonwealth would be fundamentally altered. From this there came into being a new commonwealth that, while ruled temporally by the emperor, was under the eternal Lordship of Jesus Christ, whose body was the Church, not the emperor or empire.

The Church's understanding of its relationship to the empire is consistent with this interpretation. The Church, Schmemann continues, viewed itself primarily as a "sacramental organism" whose function was "to reveal,

11. Leithart, *Defending Constantine*, 66–67.
12. Ibid., 331.
13. Ibid., 328.

manifest, and communicate the Kingdom of God, to communicate it as Truth, Grace, and Communion with God. . . . [The Church claim[ed] no 'power' in this world and ha[d] no 'earthly' interests to defend."[14] Thus, it was not difficult for the Church to leave to the state even the "'management' of her earthly life, the care and administration of her earthly needs . . . as long as the empire placed itself under Christ's judgment and in the perspective, essential for the Church, of the Kingdom of God." Schmemann continues, "The Church saw no reason to claim any 'juridical' independence from it, and, in fact gladly put the reins of ecclesiastical government and policy in the hand of the emperor."[15] In this respect, the Church's attitude toward the state was the same before Constantine as after him, rooted "precisely in the same 'eschatological ecclesiology.'"[16]

In his early work *The Historical Road of Eastern Orthodoxy*, Schmemann pauses to explain that lamentably the Justinian ideology of *symphonia* also invited a serious misconstruing of the nature of the Church. This is exemplified in the famous analogy of body and soul, such that the state is analogized as the body of the empire and the Church its soul. This analogy threatened to spiritualize the Church and render it incapable of holding a real place as a separate institution in the secular realm. "The early Church felt it was itself a body,"[17] Schmemann observes. The danger in the *symphonia* theory was that the state would not recognize the Church as a distinct community apart from the empire.[18]

In other words, there was in the Byzantine political theology always the tendency to leave little or no room for the Church to be something more than merely a spiritual or mystical entity. And in this respect, there is more than a smidgeon of truth in Gerhardt Ladner's observation that from the late fourth century onward the emperors increasingly asserted "a quasi-sacerdotal position in the Church," as the balance of influence tipped from the ascetic and mystic toward the ruler.[19]

14. Schmemann, *Church, World, Mission*, 38, 39.
15. Ibid., 40.
16. Ibid.
17. Schmemann, *Historical Road*, 150.
18. In this early work, Schmemann is quite negative about the Justinian theory of *symphonia*. He judged that this theory threatened to dissolve the Church into the empire. When he returned to this subject in *Church, World, Mission*, his mind shifted to a more positive view of the Jusitnian synthesis, though it also is clear he did not entirely abandon his earlier criticisms.
19. Gerhardt B. Ladner, *The Idea of Reform: Its Impact on Christian Thought and*

Schmemann is aware of this. He maintains that when the Church "opposed the empire, [she] did it not because of any political or social principles, not for the sake of any political doctrine of the state, but uniquely in the name of Christ whom God made the Kyrios of creation." He continues: "In other terms, she opposed the demonic 'misuse' of the state by the 'prince of this world,' [yet] her very refusal to acknowledge the emperor as Kyrios implied . . . a positive attitude towards the state, faith in the possibility for the Messiah to be accepted by the entire 'house of Israel.'"[20]

Schmemann reminds his readers that exorcism was a crucial language of the early Church and way of thinking about her presence in the world. The exercise of exorcism thus reveals how the Church interpreted the conversion of the emperor and the empire. "The power of the Cross—the Church's essential weapon against the demons—liberated the empire from the power of the 'prince of this world.' By crushing the idols, it made the empire 'open' to the Kingdom, available as its servant and instrument,"[21] and not its master. One might add that every baptism that the Church performs would hereafter be visible sign of this liberation.[22]

In a similar vein, McGuckin explains that even chapter 13 of the book of Revelation that so often is referenced as a condemnation of kingship and empire is not quite that. "Revelation demonises the earthly king who stands against the will of God and refuses to align himself with the royal King's policies for the world—the Kingdom of God. It is abundantly clear, however, that the idea the earthly ruler is either the agent of God or the servant of the beast, is prevalent throughout the entire book, and underlies all its notion of Kingship."[23]

Schmemann, Meyendorff, and McGuckin share a distinctive Orthodox ecclesiology that shapes their respective analyses. "The Church, to be sure, is *institution*"—note the absence of the article "a"—"but of *sacramental*, and not *juridical*, nature," Schmemann explains. The Church exists as institution not to wield power. Rather, it is a *presence*, the presence of the kingdom of God, in order "to assure the Church's 'passage' from 'this world'

Action in the Age of the Fathers, rev. ed. (New York: Harper and Row, 1967) 124–25.

20. Schmemann, *Church, World, Mission*, 36.

21. Ibid.

22. There are several lengthy prayers of exorcism at the beginning of the Byzantine baptismal rite.

23. McGuckin, "Legacy," 263.

into 'the world to come,' as the sign constantly to be fulfilled, as the 'means' by which the Church becomes all the time 'that which she is.'"[24]

Just how does this work out in the Byzantine doctrine of *symphonia*? It is essential for the Church, as "*sign* and *sacrament*, to be an institution." Nevertheless, its institutional features are not its *esse*, its very being. As *institution* the Church belongs to and participates in this world, however, as *fulfillment*, that is to say, in her sacramental and eschatological existence, the Church is "the world to come." There is not a division or distinction between the Church as "institution" and the Church as "fulfillment," or between "visible" and "invisible" Church; for the entire purpose of the institution is precisely to make fulfillment possible, to reveal as present that which is "to come."[25]

Thus, if we do speak of two realms or kingdoms within this Byzantine political theology, we must be careful not to confuse this distinction between two realms with Gelasius's theory of two swords, especially in its later form as developed by the scholastics, or Luther's two realms. Christ certainly testifies to two realms when, in response to Pilate, he proclaims that his kingdom is not of this world (John 18:36). But that is just it. These two realms are not comparable; one is on a strictly temporal plane and the other on an eschatological plane. Clearly, there is an earthly institution that rules over this world. That is the empire. The Church makes no claim whatsoever to fill that role. To reiterate, the Church's calling is "to witness to the anticipated presence" (i.e., the inbreaking) of the eschatological kingdom of God, "in the midst of a fallen world."[26]

To reiterate, from the standpoint of this ecclesiology, the standard description of the Byzantine system as caesaropapism misleads. Leithart rightly rejects this terminology He argues persuasively that Constantine did not intend to establish such a regime. In my view, it might be more accurate to say that caesaropapism is the perversely inverted image of the relationship of Church and empire that developed in the West. I say this because the charge of caesaropapism assumes that Church and state both behave and define themselves in terms of power, either sacerdotal or secular.

---

24. Schmemann, *Church, World, Mission*, 39.
25. Ibid.
26. Meyendorff, *Imperial Unity*, 20.

Conclusion

Peter Leithart concludes *Defending Constantine* with a provocative chapter titled "Rome Baptized." The metaphor may be misleading, but the point he is making is important. In order to explain, it helps to cite another Orthodox hymn, this one from the Christmas cycle:

> When Augustus reigned alone upon earth, the many kingdoms of men came to an end: and when Thou wast made man of the Pure Virgin, the many gods of idolatry were destroyed. The cities of the world passed under one single rule; and the nations came to believe in one sovereign Godhead. The peoples were enrolled by the decree of Caesar; and we, the faithful, were enrolled in the Name of the Godhead, when Thou, our God, was made man. Great is Thy mercy; glory to Thee.

In light of this text, the importance of Constantine's baptism to the Byzantine imagination and political theology comes clear. By his baptism, by being "enrolled in in the Name of the Godhead," the emperor joins all those who denounce the prince of this world and "the many gods of idolatry." By virtue of his baptism, the emperor also becomes a participant in the eucharistic sacrifice. This means that those "enrolled in the Name of the Godhead" henceforward have as their earthly monarch someone who owes his allegiance to the true Lord of the Cosmos and founder of the *Pax Romana*. The hymn proclaims, "The cities of the world passed under one single rule; and the nations came to believe in one sovereign Godhead."

As told by Eusebius, Constantine received baptism on his deathbed. Quite deliberately, he set aside his purple vestment for good and donned a white baptismal gown. In his final speech to Eusebius and the other bishops, Constantine stated that should his life continue, he would "associate with the people of God and unite with them in prayer as member of his church," and follow "such a course of life as befits . . . service to God."[27] Symbolically, Constantine died as a Christian neophyte, not as emperor, on the day of Pentecost in May 337. Later on, this symbolism was continued in the monastic tonsure that dying emperors received. Meyendorff comments that from the Church's point of view "with Constantine, the emperor fulfilled his mission with a full understanding of the ultimate goal of creation which was anticipated in the mysteries of the Church."[28]

---

27. Eusebius, *Life of Constantine* 4.62 (NPNF² 1:556).
28. Meyendorff, *Imperial Unity*, 30.

Thus according to both contemporary Orthodox writers and Byzantine festal hymns, Constantine's baptism signifies that the title of *Kyrios* belongs unambiguously to Christ, and that his Kingdom is not interchangeable with the empire. In spite of Eusebius's idealized portrait of the office of emperor and of Constantine himself, the Church more often than not accepted the practical reality that this "fallen world could not be changed overnight by imperial legislation." Yet the Church also took great hope from Constantine's baptism that, "the ultimate goal—the Kingdom of God—was ... common to both the Empire and the Church."[29]

In the mind of the Church, through Constantine's baptism, the empire was itself called to accept Christ, and became the wardrobe of Christ's *politeuma* in this world, This is how the Orthodox Church has understood the conversion of Constantine and the new world, the new *ecumene*, which he brought into existence. This belief did not produce a theory of separation of Church and state, with which we are so familiar in America and almost instinctively accept as a given of how these bodies ought to be related within society. Rather, the Byzantine political theology rests in an eschatological vision that, far from being limited to the salvation of the individual soul, embraces the whole of the *politeuma*. There should be no suspicion here of pietism. Indeed, this is quite the opposite of pietism.

Last, Leithart maintains that while Constantine may have believed that "he was erecting a new civic cult, a new more effective priestly college, a patriotic religious institution that would secure the *pax Dei* for Rome, Constantine was mistaken." Leithart argues that the "church is not a cult but a polis." Thus, despite the Church's "very real peccability and fallibility," the Church remains "*Christ's* city, his body, . . . [and] therefore it cannot finally be co-opted."[30] Once again, this sort of explanation echoes a Western debate that simply did not arise in the East, and should not be thought of as a key to solving the puzzles of Constantine or Byzantium.

The sharp distinction Leithart draws between cult and polity makes no sense in an Orthodox context. Isn't the Church really something of both? This certainly is how the Byzantine theology understood the matter. The Church is a special kind of "cult," as well as a special form of "polity." In service to God's redemptive purpose, the Byzantine Church adopted secular institutional forms, such as diocese, eparchy, and exarchate, that it might merge itself into one politico-ecclesiastical organism over which the

---

29. Ibid.
30. Leithart, *Defending Constantine*, 331

emperor was head, yet in no manner of speaking a priest. The Church, as "polity," as institutional structure, is, however, a presence, not a *potestas*, or power.

The initial act of the Church is to constitute itself, its *esse* or being, through a cultic act of worship. The Church is the "cult" of the Lordship of Jesus Christ, manifesting and testifying to the presence of the heavenly "polity" of the kingdom of God in in the person of Jesus Christ. It is under this same person's Lordship that the emperor places himself and his realm. Nevertheless, the "cult's" worship is not limited to a single place or time, but reaches all places and times. "Jesus said, 'Woman, believe Me, the hour is coming, when you will neither on this mountain, nor in Jerusalem, worship the Father. . . . [T]he hour is coming, and now is, when the true worshippers will worship the Father in spirit and truth; for the Father is seeking such to worship Him" (John 4:21, 23 NKJV). Christ called Constantine, and through him the empire, into the Church's service (*leiturgia*), and the empire itself became, by virtue of the Church's continuing worship of the Lord Jesus Christ, a sign and location of the presence of the eschatological *politeuma*, the kingdom of Heaven.

In Philippians, Saint Paul announces, "But our commonwealth [*politeuma*] is in heaven, and from it we await a Savior, the Lord Jesus Christ, who will change our lowly body to be like his glorious body, by the power which enables him even to subject all things to himself" (Phil 4:20–21 RSV). The Byzantine political theology, for which the Orthodox Church gives Constantine credit, rests in this truth.

If this account is accurate, then the Byzantine Church took a different path from the Roman Catholic Church and the churches of the Reformation. Its path was lit by an eschatological and sacramental vision for which the chief terms are church and world, not church and state. While the Western error lies in a juridicism that articulates a dyad of two institutions in uneasy alliance, the East's error lies in an overestimation of its eschatological hope that the Church through its worship can not only reveal the presence of the kingdom of God, but also bring about a transformation of the worldly instrumentalities of the state into ligaments of the kingdom of God. If we must use the metaphor, the latter is the true Constantinianism.

4

Evil and the Principalities
Disarming the Demonic

Cynthia L. Rigby

Introduction and Thanks

Let me begin by thanking everyone for the kind invitation I have been extended in being here, today. I am excited about exploring the important theme of "Life Amid the Principalities." As someone who teaches, most often, in Presbyterian churches, I confess I don't hear much talk either about the principalities or about the demonic. But it is language I heard and used growing up with more Anabaptist influences. And it is language that makes sense to me to use, in a different way, now, in relation to the conditions in which we find ourselves in the United States, two decades into the new millennium. I would characterize these conditions as being shaped by global capitalism, which has systematically turned our life together in this world into a series of consumeristic transactions. In this world, for example, liberal arts too often fail because we are forgetting that we love to learn for learning's sake. The point of cramming classes in the spaces of our lives is to earn credits toward degrees that will lead to a paying or better paying job. Otherwise, we reason, how can we justify making the investment? Churches are declining, I think, in part because we have turned the gospel into something understandable in the course of trying to make it more marketable. God has done "x," so the least we can do is "y"; the doctrine of grace is imagined not as God sharing with us "all that God has"[1] as much as God treating us "much better than we deserve."[2] Meanwhile, the numbers of the religiously unaffiliated grow, and the "Nones" are telling us they are tired of religion that is so judgmental and of church folks who rarely seem to practice what they preach. As it turns out, we really aren't very good at earning our salvation, or even living up to it. Maybe, as Phyllis Tickle suggests, we need another Reformation.[3]

This presentation is about "disarming the demonic," when the demonic is understood as that which stands in the way of people knowing the Gospel of grace. I will be trying, in the development of these comments, to in some way reconcile the personification of evil and principalities (that was the theology of my childhood) with my strong convictions (as a Reformed theologian) that God is one, and that God is sovereign. This reconciliation is (at least I hope!) not for the purpose of me using you to process some of my unresolved theological issues. It is rather the case that, I will argue, the demonic is successfully disarmed neither by positing personifications of evil rivals to God nor by eschewing concrete ways of naming evil by appeal to the divine sovereignty. In my view, Reformed people of faith would benefit from conceptualizing the demonic more concretely, and can do so without compromise to their convictions about the character of God's power. I will develop this thesis in four sections: First, I will talk about how to name evil before the sovereign God. Second, I will explore the relationship between evil and the demonic. Third, I will talk about how to identify the demonic in relationship to the "principalities" present in our lives. And fourth, I will conclude by discussing how to fight the demonic.

---

1. This reflects what the father says to the elder son in Luke 15:31.
2. From the Contemporary English Version Bible translation of Eph 2:8.
3. See, for example, Phyllis Tickle's *The Great Emergence: How Christianity Is Changing and Why* (Grand Rapids: Baker, 2012).

1. Naming Evil before the Sovereign God

Rulers and ruling institutions have commonly claimed they are utilizing the power of God to justify their authority. Kings, whether kind or abusive, have claimed they rule by divine right. Presidents have frequently convoluted their people's *trust in God* and *God's presence with them* as implying *they are in the right*. Religious leaders, whether sane or crazy, have said they are acting in obedience to what God has called them to do.

The identification of a ruler's power with the power of God is rarely questioned by those who benefit from the way the power is used. Those who are harmed by rulers and ruling institutions naturally reject the idea that those who are hurting them are empowered by God, often naming the abusive rulers, or at least their behavior, as "evil."

A question that quickly emerges is where the evil associated with abusive rulers and institutions comes from. Is it inherent to them, ignited by sin? Is there some kind of force in play, some kind of substantive entity affecting them? Influencing them? Causing them to use power for harm? I remember, twenty-five years ago, receiving a letter from a friend married to someone who worked very closely with the first President Bush. He was concerned, he said, about the word *evil* being applied to the then-powerful Noriega, military dictator of Panama. Can you remember the ways Noriega was abusing his people, back in 1989? My friend wanted to know if there is ever a time when we can say a person is evil. "Isn't it only the things they do that can be labeled 'evil'?," he asked. While I shared my friend's suspicion that saying someone is "evil" seems over the line, I wanted to be able to say something more than that Noriega acted badly, or even that he was turned in the wrong direction, away from the goodness of God and toward that which is not. I wanted to be able to say there is some kind of force at work that was twisting Noriega in insidious knots, but without letting Noriega off the hook for what he had done.

Christians believe it is God who is actively guiding our leaders when they do good, lead wisely, and otherwise serve their people. There are ministers gathered in this room right now who would testify that, in their very best pastoral moments, there is something more going on than just themselves and the persons to whom they are ministering. God is especially present, in the person of the Spirit, in the presence of Christ, nurturing and guiding. Giving life, mending and shaping lives. This doesn't take away from the fact that it is the minister, in all of her or his giftedness, who is ministering. But it does remind us that when Christian leaders "will and work for God's good purpose" it is because they are "enabled" to do so "by the God who works in them."[4] Similarly, Christians have held that civil leaders who lead in ways that protect and nurture the people they serve are also empowered by God. Again, they are themselves to be praised for their just and responsible acts of leadership. But we hold at the same time that there is something more than what they can accomplish themselves that is funding their good work.

Sometimes, I have to admit, it would be helpful to be able to name a kind of parallel (though less powerful) being who influences leaders and institutional systems that do harm. This is because, frankly, the evils that a person like Noriega, or an organization like Boko Haram, or a person like Dylann Roof perpetrates, seem so beyond comprehension it is hard to attribute them solely to humans while at the same time still believing human beings are created in the image of God.

And yet: from the perspective of the Reformed Christian tradition, positing that there is a sentient, substantive, and/or volition being that influences oppressive leaders and structures is problematic for a least a couple of reasons. First, because it compromises on the sovereignty of God. To say that God is the sovereign ruler of all things is to say that God has no rivals—certainly there is no being capable of doing damage to God's goodness or thwarting God's will. If there were, it would not only be the divine sovereignty that would be disrespected, but monotheism itself.

But there is a second reason why positing an evil entity is problematic. If the first is because such an idea compromises on God's singular power, the second is that it compromises on human power and agency. If there were an entity whom we could blame for the destructive dynamics of institutions and rulers, we would be sorely tempted to abdicate taking responsibility ourselves. "The devil made me do it" might become too handy of a way for us to excuse our complicity in the destructive energies of the principalities.

But here we begin to get a little stuck. I have said that positing an evil entity is problematic because it compromises on both divine and human agency. But denying that evil actually has substance can quickly (if inadvertently) lead to the diminishing or rejection of the suffering caused by oppressive structures. Since God is the sovereign author of all things, the reasoning might go, and since everything God created must be good

4. Phil 2:13

because God made it, things must not be as awful as they seem. Oh, they certainly look bad, theologians admit, and it is hard on us to endure them. But Calvin (for example) argues that we nonetheless should commit to enduring them, trusting that God has some "secret" or "hidden" plan, when matters seem to have gone awry.[5] Leibniz later explains that, really, this must be "the best of all possible worlds" given that God made it and God is both good and all-powerful.[6] And Barth suggests, following Augustine's line of thinking, that evil is the "non-real reality" that can have a genuine hold on us, but need not have this hold because it is consistent neither with God's creative nor redemptive will.[7]

But theologians such as James Cone and James Evans have argued that it is not enough to define evil as the absence of good, or as the non-real. It is not enough to use only "extraneous philosophical norms," when speaking of evil, according to Evans.[8] Cone defines evil, over against Augustine's definition, as "a power independent of the human will." But Cone consistently reminds us that "the weight of the biblical view of suffering is not on the origin of evil but on what God in Christ has done about evil . . . God became human in Jesus Christ, and defeated decisively the power of sin, death, and Satan, thereby bestowing upon us the freedom to struggle against suffering which destroys humanity."[9]

In order to engage the struggle, it is essential that we identify and condemn quite explicitly the unjust systems that perpetuate the abuse of some by others, according to Cone, Evans, and others. To *not* name distorted principalities and powers by thinking of them only in the abstract actually feeds their power. It is only when naming them substantively that we can envision standing prophetically against them. As Professor Dumbledore tells Harry Potter, when Harry is trying to avoid saying the name of the

---

5. This is a frequent argument made by Calvin throughout his work, but especially in his *Institutes of the Christian Religion*. For more on my critical reading of Calvin's appeal to the "secret will of God," see "Providence and Play," *Insights: The Faculty Journal of Austin Presbyterian Theological Seminary* 126 (2011) 10–18.

6. Gottfried Leibniz, *Theodicy* (Lasalle, IL: Open Court, 1985; first published in 1710).

7. Karl Barth uses this terminology throughout his *Church Dogmatics*, trans. G. W. Bromiley (Edinburgh: T. & T. Clark, 1956–75). See, for example, *CD* 3/1:130–32.

8. James H. Evans, *We Have Been Believers: An African-American Systematic Theology* (Minneapolis: Fortress, 1992) 8.

9. James Cone, *The God of the Oppressed* (Maryknoll, NY: Orbis, 1997) 160.

evil Voldemort, "Always use the proper name for things. Fear of a name increases fear of a thing itself."[10]

The "upside," then, to envisioning evil in relation to a distant entity—perhaps the devil, or a group of demons—is that then there is something we can face and contend with. In the world of Hogwarts, one finds the resources to confront Voldemort. Cone mentions that the "otherworldliness" of black religious traditions, often viewed with suspicion by whiter "mainline" churches, gives persons who are black ways of "resisting the demonic in their midst."[11] While Harry Potter himself faces evil, dies, and returns to life, however, we have a Savior who has done this on our behalf. Jesus Christ is the victor over the principalities and powers that would separate us from the love of God. As we sometimes sing,

> And though this world, with devils filled,
> should threaten to undo us,
> we will not fear, for God has willed
> God's truth to triumph through us.
> The Prince of Darkness grim,
> we tremble not for him.
> His rage we can endure,
> for lo, his doom is sure.
> One little word shall fell him.[12]

Note that these lyrics, penned by Martin Luther, draw not only from Psalm 46 but also from a *"christus victor"* model of atonement that is more commonly invoked by those who have been victimized by systemic injustice than by those who have been perpetrators of it. I can reference an exception to this that I think will resonate: on the Sunday after 9/11, Christians of all persuasions sang this hymn with great gusto. I guest preached that Sunday at a very white, very privileged Presbyterian Church. We sang the hymn at that service, and I don't believe I have ever heard it sung with more affect.

Having taken seriously the charge to name evil concretely, I need now to return to the complicating concern I raised earlier, namely, that once we

---

10. J. K. Rowling, *Harry Potter and the Sorcerer's Stone* (New York: Scholastic, 1997) 298.

11. James Cone, *The Cross and the Lynching Tree* (Maryknoll, NY: Orbis, 2011) 139–40.

12. "A Mighty Fortress Is Our God," Hymn #275, *Glory to God: The Presbyterian Hymnal* (Louisville: Westminster John Knox, 2013).

treat this entity that Christ has defeated as substantive, we run the risk of compromising on our monotheistic convictions. Shall we go through this life with the belief that there is one God who is good and who will undoubtedly win the war in the end, but is fighting real battles with some evil entity, day by day, in the meantime? I wonder if we might benefit from retrieving some of the otherworldly, *christus victor*, demon language without going so far as to imagine that God has any real rivals, even in the short term. Perhaps the demon language could effectively name substantive rivals *to God*, but *our* very substantive rivals. Perhaps the language of "demons" and "Satan" could be used to name the substantive principalities and powers that stand in the way of our claiming and living into the victory accomplished by Christ.

In exploring this option, I want to make sure I do not reduce the "principalities" to "personal demons"—the "chattering monkeys" that keep us from being who we really are, as created in the image of God and redeemed in Christ. Most often they are "secondary effects" of the principalities and powers and cannot be done away with without challenging the principalities and powers themselves. They come, in fact, when principalities and powers force upon us a twisted sense of who we should be and how we fit into an oppressive system that robs from the less powerful and gives to the more powerful. For example, a woman who is a member of a church that does not ordain women and is dominated by male leadership can do a lot of important spiritual work on rebuking her personal demon of low confidence, developing her theological skills, and speaking up more in Bible studies and church meetings. But until the ecclesial system that privileges the gifts of men over women is changed, this will not be enough for her to experience the freedom extended to her by Christ. It is this oppressive system, functioning as a "principality," that has likely created a context in which the woman's personal demons have been born, grown, and encouraged to thrive.

When there is a cognizance that personal demons are located in a larger system that must be changed, naming them as entities can be a step toward naming principalities and powers and taking a stand against the injustices they perpetrate. For this reason, I want to mention to you a kind of "fun" resource for naming personal demons, personifying them, and in so doing no longer allowing them damaging control. It is a book by a comic artist named Lynda Barry, titled *One Hundred Demons*.[13] In it, she

---

13. Lynda Barry, *One Hundred Demons* (Seattle: Sasquatch, 2005).

shows how creatively to paint personal demons with ink from ink stones. (Her own demons include, by the way, "Dancing," "Resilience," "Hate," "Girlness," and "San Francisco.") I'm sure Barry had no intention in this, but I can't help remembering the old legend about Martin Luther, ink, and demons. As it is commonly told, Luther was in the habit of throwing his inkwell across the room at Satan, telling Satan to get lost, in the name of Christ, because he had work to do.

Again, if we are going to have the wherewithal to confront the principalities and powers that are perpetrating injustices in the world, we had better also be working on doing what it takes to name, paint, exorcise, throw inkwells at, spit at, or do whatever it takes to rid ourselves of whatever demons we may have in our own lives. This all in the name, of course, of laying claim to the "disarming" already accomplished in Christ. It is already accomplished, but there is work to be done in actualizing this victory in our lives.

2. Evil and the Demonic

How can we think about evil and the principalities in a way that does not compromise on the character of God as One and sovereign even as it names evil concretely enough that we, in Christ, can face it head on and speak prophetically against it?

Having recognized the important critique of identifying evil as "the absence of good," I propose we take a closer look at precisely this understanding, as Augustine formulated it. In my view, in fact, this definition is an essential prerequisite to naming evil concretely. This is because it reminds us, simultaneously, both that God and all God has made is utterly good and that, whatever evil is, it is an utter aberration. It has nothing to do with who God is, and nothing to do with who we are created to be. It was Augustine's conviction about these matters, following his reading of the early chapters of Genesis as well as his philosophical ruminations on the implications of believing in one God, that led him to argue that evil is not a substantive, sentient entity. Augustine's reasoning, with which I agree, is that everything created by God was created "good." It is not that angelic beings *become* evil when they fall, but that angels "fall" when they look away from their Lord toward the emptiness that is *not* God, the emptiness that is the absence of God, the emptiness Augustine called "evil." Angels, then, do not become evil, but they are affected by their looking toward evil and framing their existence accordingly. To speak of demons, it seems to me, is to have a personified, concrete way of naming the fact that a person or an institution has "turned the wrong way" and is no longer acting in relation to God, others, and the rest of the created order, but has lost sight of its own status as creaturely and good, claiming god-ness for itself.

It might be helpful, at this point, to replace the language of "evil" with the language of "the demonic." Principalities cannot be identified as evil without compromising on the character of God because they have substance, God made everything that has substance, and God made no evil. But they can be understood to have turned away from God and toward everything that is not-God, not-real, not-substantive, and not-good. When principalities and powers forget that they are creatures, and are therefore subject to limitations and correction; when they function as though they are a "god" who is beyond all question, they have become demonic. They may even be represented by demons, as long as it is understood that demons are not evil (since they have substance) but are, rather, twisted up distortions of God's creative and redemptive intentions. Like that androgynous, satanic figure in Mel Gibson's *The Passion of the Christ* (2004), those who lose sight of who they are before God get all twisted up and out of shape.

Speaking of how structures participate in "the demonic," rather than how they are ontologically "evil," gives a concrete way of naming the heinous realities we face without compromising on what we believe is the character of God and, frankly, without giving up on the possibility of transformation. Speaking of "the demonic" further calls all of us who participate in unjust systems to task because it names the fact that all who participate in such systems have in some way turned away from that which is real and true and toward that which is falsehood. To identify complicity in the demonic is to call to repentance, to a turning back to who God is and to who we really are in relationship to God.

Employing the language of the "demonic" further addresses the concern of Cone and other liberation theologians that we who define evil in philosophical terms are thinking of it in ways that are far too thin. To think of evil as "the absence of good" can seem inadequate when we are thinking of the heinous crimes perpetuated by principalities, as though they are sins of omission rather than sins of commission. Nothing could be further from the truth. To say that such actions are demonic, rather than evil, is to name the fact that they are substantive, nameable, and concrete. To name such actions as demonic is to recognize that they are as far removed from the reality of God and their good creation in the image of God as it is possible to be.

Important to naming the demonic at full strength, with the kind of concrete thickness insisted upon by Cone and others, is to be very clear about identifying evil as the complete absence of God. Such a move is counter-intuitive, for many of us who are used to emphasizing that God is with us "no matter what." This, of course, is the reassuring message of the Gospel. The problem comes when we lean on the Good News as a way of escaping the difficult work of naming and confronting injustices perpetrated by the principalities. When we merely insist that God is with us in the midst of it all, somehow working everything together for good, we have exempted ourselves from doing the hard work God may use to accomplish such transformation. Identifying the demonic so we can "call it out," however, requires also that we name the ways God is *not* present, the ways in which we can see a demonic "turning away" from that which is and a "turning toward" that which is not.

A theologian who writes brilliantly on this subject is Gustavo Gutiérrez. Interestingly, Gutiérrez is a liberation theologian who thinks privileged persons should be thinking more, not less, about the absence of God. "Whenever and wherever God's reign and demand that we 'do what is right and just' are denied," he insists, "God is not present."[14] Where Cone and Evans criticize "philosophical" approaches that understand evil to be the absence of God, Gutiérrez notes that "there is a philosophically inspired theology that has difficulty in handling the biblical assertion of God's absence."[15] Gutiérrez suggests that those of us who live in the Western world need to pay more attention to stories in the biblical witness that take seriously God's absence. For example, he says, in the book of Jeremiah God is very clear that if the people do not help the poor, God will not dwell with them in the temple.[16] Gutiérrez thinks that North Americans, in particular, are too quick to name God's presence in crises, and should give more attention to the reality of evil, the experience of God's absence that comes with a turning away from what is. Gutiérrez suggests that to too glibly invoke God's presence without being open to naming God's absence in the dynamics of the demonic is to forget that God's presence *means something*.

---

14. Gutiérrez, *God of Life*, trans. Matthew J. O'Connell (Maryknoll, NY: Orbis, 1991) 70.

15. Ibid.

16. Ibid., ch. 5, sec. 1, "God Has Departed."

It means life and not death, peace and not war, freedom and not bondage, justice and not injustice. Where there is death and war and bondage and sin, it is appropriate to cry out (as Jesus did), "Where is God?" It is appropriate for those who believe in God faithfully to confess, in the face of the ugly and oppressive influence of the principalities and powers, "No, this is not it. God is *not* here."

I thought of what I learned from Gutiérrez when that terrible school shooting occurred, back in 1999, in Columbine, Colorado. We Christians in our United States culture were so quick to look for the ways God was present in the midst of such a heinous, unthinkable event. We wanted so badly both to make the story better and to make some sense of it at all that we turned seventeen-year-old Cassie Bernall into a martyr, insisting that it was her belief in God that led to her killing. The story suggested that there was something good about the shooting, since Bernall was able to serve as a witness to the Christian faith. Later on, investigations showed that Bernall probably wasn't asked about her beliefs before she was shot, after all.

To name the principalities and powers at work in that event would not have meant abdicating belief that God is present, but rather taking the content of that presence seriously enough to say, "No, God is not there when two kids shoot and kill twelve other kids in a school library. What happened there has absolutely nothing to do with what God is about." From there we can then bear witness to incarnation—God entering into creaturely life and death in Jesus Christ; Jesus entering even into hell—into the place where God is absent. God in Jesus Christ of course entered right there, into the absence, with those kids in the library. But the radical and revolutionary character of God's entry into this world of violence and suffering is liable to be missed if we create narratives that resist naming the reality of the abyss even in those places and events where it is deepest, widest, and darkest.

3. Identifying the Demonic

How do we identify the demonic so we can name it and engage in the work of God that will disarm it? In his classic text *Moral Man and Immoral Society*, Reinhold Niebuhr raises the concern that, even when individuals can manage to turn their eyes and hearts toward God, acting accordingly, this is harder for institutions. According to Niebuhr, while it may be the case that *individuals* are moral, turning themselves and their behaviors away from evil and toward the good, it is much more difficult to imagine *institutions* turning toward the good. This is because it is impractical for them to do so—even more impractical than it would be for individuals. As Niebuhr explains it, society cannot afford idealism in the way an individual might be able to embrace it and still survive. Society needs power, and struggles for power, in order to keep running.[17]

I can see why Niebuhr would say that it is even harder to wrench institutions from the demonic than it is to turn individuals back toward God.

Thinking about what he says I remember a time, years ago, when we were beginning a self-study at Austin Seminary, where I teach. We were beginning to review our mission statement, and we had brought in a consultant to help us. She asked us questions to help us think about our identity. "Who are your competitors, and what can you do to beat them?" was one of the questions she kept asking us. The faculty didn't like this question. We told her we tried not to think in terms of competitors and beating others out. And we mainly meant it. We told her we wanted to support our sibling schools, and that we would rather think of what we had to offer that was unique than how to overwhelm the best of our competitors. Our response baffled her. What she thought was a foolproof assumption—that we wanted to gain power over and against other schools—was to her the only way of viewing the world. "It's not personal, it's just business," I remember her saying one time, trying to argue with us, quoting Donald Trump. She had no idea what to do about the fact that we didn't share her assumptions, which she never seemed to realize were arbitrary.

What's interesting about this is that, as incapable as this consultant was of steering us away from being who we are before God and toward that which we are not, she was certainly more right than we were about what we need to do to be successful, as an educational institution, in a world so consistently swayed by the demonic. I guess a question I always have, and that I think is provoked by Niebuhr, too, is how we can teach and preach grace, unconditional love, and irreplaceability, but then run our institutions and churches on the basis of rules, merit, and the manipulative, theologically incorrect aphorism that no one is irreplaceable. To live under the conditions of such a contradiction is to participate in the demonic while pretending we have superseded it; it is to be *of* the world but not actually to be *in*

---

17. See Reinhold Niebuhr, *Moral Man and Immoral Society* (Louisville: Westminster John Knox, 2001; first published in 1932).

it. Life amidst the principalities can in no way be the abundant life Christ came to bring us[18] if we ourselves are guilty of such hypocrisy.

Living authentically as those who resist the demonic clearly takes a good deal of effort. It begins, as mentioned earlier, with the identification and naming of that which is abhorrent. How do we identify the demonic that is alive and well on planet earth? Several theologians offer descriptions that can help us name it for what it is and begin to take a stand against it, both personally and corporately. Karl Barth, for example, instructs us look to where power is operative apart from any accountability, when it is leveraged only for its own sake rather than for the purpose of bringing life. His favorite term for the demonic is "lordless powers," and he sees these powers operative in all forms of political absolutism as well as in all instances in which money or material goods are idolatrized.[19] During World War II, as a leader of the Confessing Church, he identified Hitler and others as "lordless powers" who claim to govern the world but who are living a delusion, given that Jesus Christ is the only Messiah, the only Lord.[20]

Interestingly, Barth understands there to be quite a range of "lordless powers." At the end of his life in the late 1960s, for example, he writes about "fashion" as a "lordless power." His concern seems to be that women feel it necessary to be constantly changing their wardrobe, which he thinks must distract them from seeing themselves as who they are before God. "Who wants it this way?" asks Barth. "The particular industry that tirelessly makes money out of it and whose kings, we are told, reside especially in Paris? But who has made these people the kings? What is it that has always made this industry so lucrative? . . . Who inspires and directs these processes, which are not a matter of indifference to the feeling for life and all that it implies?"[21]

While Barth would obviously not place on par the crimes of the Nazis and the crimes of the fashion industry, I think it is inspiring and challenging to note that he is looking to identify the demonic, looking to perceive the lordless powers, at all times. I wonder if it is not a kind of corollary to him always being open to receiving the Word of God, ever anew, that he would have us be simultaneously ever open to seeing what is *not* the Word

---

18. See John 10:10b.

19. See Karl Barth, *The Christian Life: Church Dogmatics IV/4; Lecture Fragments*, trans. G. W. Bromiley (Grand Rapids: Eerdmans, 1981) 213–33.

20. See "The Theological Declaration of Barmen" (1934), in *The Book of Confessions* (Louisville: Office of the General Assembly, 2007).

21. Barth, *Christian Life*, 229.

of God, what is turned in the wrong direction from the life God desires for us.

In addition to fashion, Barth considers in relationship to the "lordless powers" both transportation and technology. Earlier in his work he suggests that the stress that comes with overpacked, overextended lives veers toward the demonic, because to live as those who think there is no way to live other than to be "stressed out" is to deny that we live "before the sovereign God." When we live before the sovereign God, Barth says, in contrast to this, our work "cannot be anything but play."[22]

A less commonly known theologian who writes about identifying the demonic in relation to the principalities is William Stringfellow. Back in the 1960s Stringfellow wrote books that suggest that when we are trying to ascertain whether or not an institution we are involved in is actually veering toward the demonic (or whether it is we who are off base in our reading of it) we test to see if certain elements are present. Three of these are "the denial of truth," "doublespeak and overtalk," and "secrecy and boasts of expertise." Let me briefly elaborate on each of these three in turn.[23]

(1) *The denial of truth*: American merchandising lies all the time about what we need and what products can do, Stringfellow says, and institutions follow suit. Thinking of our own era, what immediately comes to mind is Stephen Colbert's coinage of the term "truthiness." It has become okay for us to say anything that has a gut-level ring of truth to it, even if there is no actual truth to support it. When are principalities speaking the truth, and when are they being merely truth-y? And how do we get at the difference?

(2) *Doublespeak and overtalk*: Do we hear our institutions engaging in doublespeak, that word that became known by way of Orwell's novel *1984*? "War is peace" has become the classic example. No: war is not peace. But: when it is said often enough and quickly enough, we begin to believe that it is.

(3) *Secrecy and boasts of expertise*: Do the principalities and powers that surround us discourage questions and withhold information in the name of secrecy, urging us to "trust" the expertise of our superiors? "Nowadays," writes Stringfellow in the late 1960s, "Americans are told that secrecy is an indispensable principle of government."

---

22. *Church Dogmatics*, 3/4:553.
23. William Stringfellow, *Essential Writings* (Maryknoll, NY: Orbis, 2013).

A couple of years ago Allan Boesak was visiting my institution[24] and took us to task for sitting back while American freedoms are being slowly but surely taken away by our government in the name of national security. "Do you have any idea what we have had to do to achieve these liberties in our country [South Africa]?" he asked us. "And you don't even seem to know it is happening. Once these are taken away, it will take generations to get them back," he warned. And somewhere in the recesses of my mind I could almost hear Stringfellow's list cycling: exaggeration and deception, cursing and conjuring, diversion and demoralization. I had missed the signs. I had forgotten to watch for them. And Professor Boesak was right: it was now, in some significant ways, too late.

I don't know about you, but these endless, concrete criteria offered by Stringfellow coupled with Boesak's pointed and honest warning make me realize I need to stop overlooking just how much that which is swirling around me is turned toward evil, participating in the demonic. For too long I have seen not being overly reactive as a virtue. But perhaps being even-keeled, in the face of the demonic, is actually a form of participation in it. The truth is that I cannot readily extract myself (nor the various institutions I serve) from the principalities and powers that surround us. I—and my communities—participate in the dynamics. If we are to extricate ourselves and work for change, we are going to have to put up a fight.

4. How to Fight the Demonic

And so, finally, what to do? How do we fight the demonic? How do we ourselves turn away from the absence of good that is evil and toward the good that is God, that is God's will for us?

Certainly, in relation to our own complicity there is a place and a need for repentance and for changed behavior. Part and parcel of the naming that disarms fear is being up front—through confession—about our own subscription to the demonic. We can repent of our personal involvement, and we can repent also as representatives of institutions and communities with which we are identified. As an Anglo-American person who teaches in an institution that was founded in the late nineteenth century by Dr. Robert Lewis Dabney, one of the leading proponents of the idea that the Bible

---

24. Boesak visited and lectured at Austin Seminary on October 5, 2012. This paragraph is a paraphrase of an unrecorded conversation we had at a smaller group lunch, following his lecture.

supports slavery, I cannot repent often enough of the ways in which we in our culture still turn toward evil, participating in a demonic distortion that has yet to adequately honor as created in the image of God those human beings who have darker skin. In relation to the ways in which institutions have done harm, recently or in the past, there is a place for standing up and saying, "This is wrong. This does not reflect the presence of God, but God's absence. This is contrary to God's will. This will not do. We have to turn around and face the other way."

In relation to some of the distortions that have been named, it is hard work to fight the demonic. In relation to racism. In relation to classism. In relation to sexism. There is incredible pressure imposed by institutions of all kinds, in this country, to pretend that these issues that have been mentioned rather than fully named have already been resolved. In truth, they have not. Even if there is vast improvement in some ways, there is a long way to go. How do we identify and call out the demonic in those—including ourselves—who have the very best intentions, who really want to be free of the prejudices, hate, and misunderstanding that have for so long divided us?

And then there are demonic distortions we have only begun whispering about, but have barely mentioned out loud. I think, in particular, of global capitalism. How do we look straight at the lies of merit and wealth and equal opportunity for all and "any kid can grow up and be president" and speak the truth, resisting doublespeak? How do we risk saying "no: we do not trust" to those who are asking us to trust them, to trust their expertise, but who are actually controlled by the pressure to make more money, to replace people as necessary, to lie without flinching if it means gaining power and influence? How do we take these realities on when we cannot even point to them from a distance; when we ourselves are participants in and perpetuators of the dynamics?

Barth suggests that a way we fight demonic principalities is by praying the Lord's Prayer.[25] "Deliver us from evil," we pray, remembering through our words that we are not lords of our own lives, but that "the kingdom, and the power, and the glory forever" are God's. "Thy kingdom come!" we insist, stomping our feet and asking for God to show God's power and to make it evident in every way on this earth as it is in heaven. And this imperative

---

25. For more on this subject, see Karl Barth's *Prayer*, including an essay precisely on the theme of the prayer and the "lordless powers" written by Donald McKim (Louisville: Westminster John Knox Press, 2002).

is followed up by the request that "Thy will be done." It is not simply that we are asking God to come and undo the lordless powers, defeating them in the end. It is that God calls us into God's work of transformation. We, with Christ, are privileged to work to bring God's kingdom to earth as it is in heaven.

What this finally looks like, I think, includes a lot of watching and praying. Looking out at the world, identifying the Word of God, and also identifying the lordless powers that demonically try to turn us away from the good, acceptable, and perfect will of God.[26] And what it looks like, further, is to always be ready to act—to do justice—when we see our chance. This is where I hear Boesak reminding us, again, that we need to be ready. We are called to act. We must not assume that the chances will always be there, or that they will come back in this lifetime.

May God give all of us the grace to turn, even on this day, back to the truth of the One who made us, to the One who loves us, and to the One who promises to sustain us in what really is a battle with the principalities and powers, until that day.

---

26. See Rom 12:1–2.

5

Augustine on Principalities and Powers

C. C. Pecknold

AS A PREFATORY ASIDE, I am aware of debates in New Testament scholarship that parallel my interest in Augustine on principalities and powers. Paul Hinlicky's essay in this volume also refers to these recent debates between N. T. Wright and John Barclay on whether "principalities and powers" in Paul centers around the Roman Empire or not. Wright wants to remind everyone that the ancient world didn't divide religion and politics. When Paul says "Jesus is Kurios," he is being treasonous from a Roman perspective. He is implying that Caesar is not Lord. Barclay, on the other hand, argues that Rome was not a key player on Paul's stage. He never inveighs directly against Rome (think of Revelation by way of contrast). For Paul, the enemy is "the god of this age" (2 Cor 4:4). The empire may cooperate with the Enemy, but this remains insignificant in itself. This is a fascinating debate for an Augustinian like me because for all Augustine's interest in Rome, I think he would actually side with Barclay and not Wright on this question. As Hinlicky stresses in his essay, Ephesians seems to distance the powers from human agents. Indeed, Ephesians contrasts these powers with flesh and blood (Eph 6:16) and claims that through our union with Christ even we are seated above them (Eph 2:6). We were once enslaved to them (Eph 2:2). The Colossians are trapped in a heresy the precise contours of which remain elusive but which involves interest in these same powers (Col

2:20–23). Colossians 1:15–20 shows their subservience to Christ through whom they were created. They gained power over us because of our debt of sin, but Christ conquered them and nailed the bond of debt to the cross (Col 2:9–15). In Galatians, submission to circumcision is equated with a return to these powers (Gal 4:9). Odd for a Jew to say, but say it he must: to submit to circumcision is to turn from Christ and so turn to demons. In 1 Corinthians, Paul says they killed the Lord (1 Cor 2:8) not realizing that it was their defeat. They and death itself will finally be subjected to Christ (1 Cor 15:24–26). In addition to the Pauline corpus, the language of principalities and powers is also consistently used to refer to nonhuman powers in noncanonical apocalyptic literature. My prefatory aside, then, is to simply assert that the early church fathers in general, and Augustine in particular, would incline to Barclay's rather than Wright's view that the powers and principalities phrase clearly refers (always) to nonhuman powers.[1] Arguments to the contrary would, at the very least, contradict Augustine's understanding of such powers. In a limited way, this essay aims to demonstrate that it is anachronistic to assume that powers and principalities refer in any way to civil instruments of governance for the common good.

While many theologians today have come to associate this Pauline phrase "principalities and powers" with a critique of politics, the early church fathers associated the phrase not with politics but with the wickedness and snares of the Devil. Augustine was no exception. So as someone who works in the crossroads between Augustine and contemporary theology, this antique-modern tension gives me pause. My hunch is that we moderns have divested ourselves of all patristic and medieval speculation about angels and demons (too much Bultmann, perhaps). As a result, we have reduced our theological imagination. Instead of understanding the human person in analogical relation to angelic natures, our thought is now forced analogically downwards.[2] This is also true of our theo-political imagination. Because we have excluded all patristic and medieval speculation about an-

---

1. I am grateful to Nathan Eubank for conversations about these important debates in Pauline studies which have some tangential bearing on my subject. See N. T. Wright, *Paul and the Faithfulness of God* (Minneapolis: Fortress, 2013) passim, and especially John Barclay, *Pauline Churches and Diaspora Jews* (Tübingen: Mohr Siebeck, 2011) 363–88.

2. On this point, see Serge-Thomas Bonino, *Les anges et les démons: Quatorze leçons de théologie catholique* (Paris: Parole et Silence, 2007).

gelic agency, both holy and fallen, we have reduced "powers and principalities" to mere human political agency which always must be resisted, and yet paradoxically we have also raised earthly politics to either an angelic or demonic power, a mysterious, spiritual force in human affairs. This is a profoundly modern problem, and it would strike Augustine as a kind of category mistake.

My task in this paper, all caveats aside now, is simple. My aim is to examine in more detail the imaginative framework that Augustine brings to the phrase "principalities and powers," first in light of his philosophical formation, then in light of his biblical understanding, all the while attending to his arguments in *The City of God* against Greco-Roman polytheism, and in support of his mature ecclesiological and political conclusions concerning a cosmic struggle between two cities. What I think this will demonstrate, however inadequately, is that Augustine's use of the phrase "principalities and powers" never implicates human politics directly, except by way of idolatry and false civil religion, which is to say by way of false worship and sacrifice. Augustine's analysis of Roman civic polytheism does show us, however, how an early church father was inclined to understand these nonhuman powers, and it is to this topic we turn now.

1. Of Daemons and Eudaemons: Augustine's Philosophical Sources

The *daemons* are frequently mentioned in the works of Plato, especially the *Symposium*, where they are mediators between the gods and humans. Like humans, there are good and bad daemons. Indeed, the famous Greek term for happiness, *eudaimonia*, literally means "good daemon." Augustine knows his Plato, of course, and primarily through Porphyry and Apuleius (*City* 12.25) he also knows how the Platonic tradition develops in a religious, cultic direction. Augustine's own parishioners in Hippo would have been aware of their neighbors making sacrifices to daemons for the salvation of souls. Augustine himself complains that some very confused Christian parents continued the practice of sacrificing to daemons on behalf of their baptized children! In light of this, we can understand that Augustine's extensive treatment of the daemons in *City of God* 8–10 was not simply crucial for his argument with civic polytheist revivalists, but also crucial for teaching his own parishioners.[3] Our main source for Augustine's under-

---

3. For Augustine's lament over such confused Christians, see, e.g., *Ep.* 98.1–13.

standing of the daemons is, in fact, *The City of God*, and his discussion of them is not at all arcane to his original readers, both pagan and Christian. It occurs within a two-part argument against Roman desires to return to Roman polytheism in the wake of the sack of Rome in 410.

In books 1–5 of the *City*, Augustine had argued that the Roman gods, virtues, powers, and daemons do the Roman people no temporal good, but have actually brought material harm to them as people and as a society. In books 6–10, he attempts to show how their desire to return to the gods is even more irrational when one asks about what sort of eternal or spiritual benefits the gods bring. And here is where his most extensive knowledge of the daemons occurs, as they provide him with the theme of mediation with which he will build to his climactic conclusion that Christ alone is the one true Mediator between the one God and humanity.

In book 6, Augustine mounts a concentrated philosophical argument against Varro's threefold classification of theology as political, poetic, and philosophical (or civil, mythical, and natural). There he argues that Varro rightly prefers the natural theology that inclines to world-soul monotheism over the confused, irrational, and self-refuting polytheistic rites that permeate civil and mythical theologies of the city and the theatre, but faults Varro for not seeing how the philosophical search for metaphysical causation in the world should help him to see the falsehood of Roman polytheism, which he describes as a "a bottomless pit of delirium" that degrades the people, and turns obscene degradation into a luxury and amenity (6.6). While the natural theologies of pagan scholars are also mixed with much error, and not natural enough, Augustine is keen to bracket the question of natural theology in order to demonstrate for his readers the way in which the mythical theologies of the theatre are really vehicles for civic polytheism, which has a corrosive influence on Roman souls.

Yet the theology of the philosophers comes in for criticism as well. Varro and other naturalists find many elements of the world worthy of their respect, contemplation and even worship. They identify these elements as parts of the World Soul, an emanation of the God of nature. Augustine does not immediately proclaim such natural theologians as blasphemers. Rather, he thinks they have simply made a category mistake that he doesn't seem to think they could know without divine revelation. In fact, what he says is that all of these natural principles can be predicated of the one true God. If only these natural theologians could refer to the properly transcendent cause of nature, if only they could understand these attributes of the world "to the true God, who made the world, who is the creator of every soul and every material substance," then they could properly direct their worship (7.29). Augustine had initiated an argument about the worship of the gods in book 6, but by the end of book 7 he states clearly what constitutes the proper worship of God:

> The God of our worship is he who has created all beings, and ordered the beginning and end of their existence and their motion. He has in his hands the causes of all that exists; and all those causes are within his knowledge and at his disposition. . . . It is the one true God who is active and operative in all those [natural] things, but always acting as God, that is, present everywhere in his totality, free from all spatial confinement, completely untrammeled, absolutely indivisible, utterly unchangeable, and filling heaven and earth with his ubiquitous power which is independent of anything in the natural order. He directs the whole of his creation, while allowing to his creatures the freedom to initiate and accomplish activities which are their own; for although their being completely depends on him, they have a certain independence.[4] He often acts through the medium of his angels, but he himself is the sole source of the angels' blessedness. And so, although he sends angels to men for various purposes, it is from him, not from the angels, that blessings come to men, as they come also to the angels. It is from this one true God that we hope for eternal life. (7.30)

And he continues that it is this one true God who has "sent to us his Word, who is his only Son, who was born and who suffered in the flesh which he assumed for our sake—so that we might know the value God placed on mankind, and might be purified from all our sins by that unique sacrifice, and when all difficulties have been surmounted, we may come to eternal rest and to the ineffable sweetness of the contemplation of God" (7.31). It is against this backdrop of real transcendence that Augustine then says that while philosophy is capable of going a great distance in unmasking the weakness of civic polytheistic theologies, only the one true religion has "the power to prove that the gods of the nations are unclean demons," has the power to set human beings free from their temptations (7.33). The unmasking and overcoming of the powers, for Augustine, is not the overcoming of imperial politics (indeed, Augustine praises Constantine and Theodosius

---

4. The importance of this text for understanding both Augustine and the Catholic Church's teaching on the "legitimate autonomy" of politics is frequently neglected.

alike), rather it is the unmasking and overcoming of not only polytheism, but the demonic influence deceiving the human mind and soul (7.35).

The Argument of *City* 8–10

Varro's failures at natural theology—namely his inability to distinguish God from the world, to see beyond the visible world—does not settle the question of the philosopher's worship. In books 8 and 9, Augustine finally ascends to the Platonic tradition that he most admires. For "these thinkers acknowledge a God who transcends any kind of soul, being the maker not only of this visible world—heaven and earth, in the familiar phrase—but also of every soul whatsoever, a God who gives blessedness to the rational and intelligent soul—the class to which the human soul belongs—by giving it a share in his unchangeable and immaterial light. Those philosophers are classed Platonists . . ." (8.1). His praise for the Platonists is well known. He writes, "If Plato says that the wise man is the man who imitates, knows and loves this God, and that participation in this God brings man happiness, what need is there to examine the other philosophers? There are none who come nearer to us than the Platonists. Platonism must take pride of place over 'fabulous' theology, with its titillation of impious minds by rehearsing the scandals of the gods, and over 'civil' theology, where unclean demons, posing as gods, have seduced the crowds . . ." (8.5). The Platonists are not only superior to the civil and mythical theologies, but also to the natural theology of Varro who did not understand that the true God is author of the universe, the source of the world rather than constituted by it. These true philosophers could rise from the perceptible realities of nature to the invisible, intelligible realities that caused them. Augustine praises their rational demonstrations of the simplicity, immutability and unchangeable nature of God, and their ability to distinguish the created and derivative from the uncreated and underivative.

2. Christ the One True Sacrifice and Mediator

The culmination of the argument against the daemons builds to a powerful christological argument about sacrifice and mediation at the end of book 9 and the beginning of book 10. The daemons have an intermediate position between gods and men, but that makes them neither happy nor wretched, neither mortal nor immortal; they have the attributes of eternity but they are susceptible to the passions (9.13). These *daemons*, in other words, are not *eu*daimons—they are not happy, they are miserable because they cannot really unite us in our mortality to the immortal and eternal good. Augustine says that many of these Platonic philosophers have asked whether one can be both mortal and happy, and have been divided on the question. He asks, if there were such people who could be both mortal and happy, who envy no one, who embody the virtues and attain happiness in all things, then why wouldn't they become mediators, or why wouldn't they join the company of the happy angels? Augustine responds that "the more credible and probable position is that . . . we must look for a mediator who is not only human but also divine, so that men may be brought from mortal misery to blessed immortality by the intervention of the blessed mortality of this mediator" (9.15).

The daemons are bad mediators who separate friends, whereas Christ is a very different kind of mediator, one who reconciles enemies (9.15). Why do bad mediators separate? Because that is the logic of the evil angels who turned away from participation in the one God from the beginning—and so were deprived of happiness. No, Augustine writes, "that good which can bring happiness" is not the good which the many bad mediators can bring, but which only Christ the one Mediator can bring to us, "and that one Mediator in whom we can participate and by participation reach our felicity, is the uncreated Word of God, by whom all things were created" (9.15). This is the good mediation we humans need, that "God himself, the blessed God who is the giver of blessedness" would become "partaker of our nature and thus [offer] us a short cut to participation in his own divine nature . . . the Trinity, in which the angels participate, and so achieve their felicity" (9.15). We need a mediator who becomes truly one with us, yet who can help purify, heal and free us from sin and defilement. And Augustine confesses that God has done this in his incarnation. Indeed, what his incarnation shows us is that his divine nature cannot be polluted even by taking on our sin and defilement, and secondly, that demons have no power over us (9.17). This is the culmination of his argument about the demons, namely that they have been disarmed. Indeed, they are puffed up with nothing, like balloons without substance. They are a kind of "windy emptiness" in their arrogance, they make claims to power that can only be due to the one true God, and in response to this puffed up power, this counterfeit knowledge they offer to humans, is contrasted "the humility of God, revealed in Christ" (9.20). Here the power of God is manifested, and the demons make their customary deflationary flight from his presence. Augustine points to the demons who ask Jesus, in Mark 1:24, "What business have you with us, Jesus the Nazarene? Have you come to destroy us?" And he observes that their question shows their true nature is fear of losing their own power of existence. Rather, Augustine says that God's purpose is not to reveal the demons to us, but "to free us from their tyrannical power," which is really not a power at all to those who are not deceived, to those who participate in the eternal power and wisdom of God (9.21). Christ allowed himself to be tempted by the prince of the demons only to demonstrate that they were under his control, that they had no power over Christ, and so reveal to us that they have no such power. After the temptation, it was similarly clear that the good and holy angels ministered to Christ, and wherever Christ went, he excited the fears of impure spirits, none of whom could resist his commands (9.21).

3. The Creation of the Angels: Augustine's Biblical Angelogy

From the Apostle Paul, Augustine knows that angels can be classified as angels, archangels, thrones, dominions, powers, principalities, virtues, and that they can come in groups such as choirs and legions. He considers the angelic appearances of named angels, such as Gabriel who appeared to Mary (Luke 1:19), Lucifer (Isa 14:12), and Michael (Jude 9), as well as unnamed angels, such as the one appearing to Joseph, or the several who appeared at the tomb of Christ, or the seven angels of the apocalypse, the angels of the seven churches (Rev 8:2).[5] His most extensive discussion of angels, in fact, occurs in *City of God* 11–12 where he is especially concerned to understand the creation of the angels as constituting a cosmic, spiritual origin for the two cities.

The Argument of *City* 11–12

When Augustine shifts his argument to the scriptural narrative in books 11–22, he seeks to show the history of the two cities in terms of their origins (11–14), histories (15–18), and destinies (19–22). It should come as no

---

5. See Frederick Van Fleteren, "Angels," in *Augustine Through the Ages: An Encyclopedia*, ed. Allan D. Fitzgerald et al. (Grand Rapids: Eerdmans, 1999) 20–22.

surprise by now that he finds the origin of the two cities not in the human fall but in the angelic fall, and so, he writes, "I have decided that I must first deal with the subject of the holy angels. They form the greater part of that City, and the more blessed part, in that they have never been on pilgrimage in a strange land" (11.9). He admits that the creation of the angels is not treated explicitly in Genesis, but for a variety of textual reasons he concludes that the angels are created, and they are created at that point at which God said *Fiat lux*: "Let there be light." Augustine writes,

> For when God said, "Let there be light," and light was created, then, if we are right in interpreting this as including the creation of the angels, they immediately become partakers of the eternal light, which is the unchanging Wisdom of God, the angent of God's whole creation; and this Wisdom we call the only begotten Son of God. Thus the angels, illuminated by that light by which they were created, themselves became light, and are called "day," by participation in the changeless light and day, which is the Word of God, through whom they themselves and all other things were made. This is "the true light, which illuminates every man as he comes into the world"; and this light illuminates every pure angel, so that he is not light in himself, but in God. If an angel turns away from God he becomes impure: and such are all those who are called "impure spirits." They are no longer "light in the Lord"; they have become in themselves darkness, deprived of participation in the eternal light. For evil is not a positive substance; the loss of good has been given the name of "evil." (11.9)

Augustine immediately affirms that God is simple, unchangeable, and that the "subsistent Persons" of the Trinity are truly one God in order to emphasize the way in which God's essence and his existence are identical, whereas creatures have a derived existence, and this includes angelic and human natures whose attributes can only be perfected through participation in the changeless Wisdom of God.

Pure angels derive their light from the immaterial light of the simple Wisdom of God. "But" Augustine writes, "there were some angels who turned away from this illumination, and so did not attain to the excellence of a life of wisdom and bliss, which must of necessity be eternal, and certainly assured of its eternity" (11.11). This presents a difficulty for Augustine. Participation in the eternal happiness of God is irresistible, and so in order to allow for a turning away, Augustine speculates that the angels were created in a beatitude fitting to their own nature, but not the summit of happiness which was possible for them. As he puts it, "For we do not confine the word 'beatitude' within such narrow limits of connotation as to ascribe it only to God, although he is so truly blessed that no greater beatitude is possible" (11.11). Though Augustine himself does not develop the kind of celestial hierarchy that a Christian Platonist like Dionysius the Pseudo-Areopagite will, he does articulate a principle that would immediately admit such hierarchical speculation about the beatitude proper to divine, angelic, and human nature.[6] The point is that being created for "the endless enjoyment of God Most High," which is true freedom, does not mean possession of that happiness at the point of creation, and this is what the Devil cannot abide. In Johannine terms, Augustine insists that "the Devil sins from the beginning" (1 John 3:8), but this cannot mean that he sinned from the first moment of his creation. Augustine thinks that would be a Manichean claim, for if the Devil sinned by nature then there could be "no question of sin," there could be no angelic fall (11.15). Augustine is sure that God made the Devil, but equally sure that he did not make him wicked. Rather, what "sins from the beginning" means is that "from the beginning of his own creation the Devil did not stand fast in the truth, and for that reason he never enjoyed felicity with the holy angels, because he refused to be subject to his creator, and in his arrogance supposed that he wielded power as his own private possession and rejoiced in that power. . . . He has refused to accept reality and in his arrogant pride presumes to counterfeit an unreality" (11.13). In this way, Augustine sounds out one of his clarion themes that the Devil is the first to fall from the truth precisely because he cannot abide a participated existence in the supreme good that is God. The word he almost always uses to describe this refusal to receive his existence from God is *superbia* (11.15). As everyone knows, Augustine has set himself the arduous task in *The City of God* to convince the proud of the excellence of humility (Preface). And here Augustine brings his readers to the cosmic mystery of why pride stands at the self-defeating origin of a potency for division, darkness, sin and death.

One of the surprising upshots of this discussion of the Devil in book 11 is to make a basic theological claim about the fundamental goodness of nature, and about locating the mysterious origins of sin in choice. As he

---

6. See Pseudo-Dionysius, "The Celestial Hierarchy," in *Complete Works*, trans. Colm Luibheid (New York: Paulist, 1987) 143–92. As well, consider the importance of St. Thomas Aquinas as "the Angelic Doctor," which is due to the considerable place he gives to angelology in the *Summa Theologiae* (esp. Ia. 50–64), where he draws heavily from both Augustine and Pseudo-Dionysius.

puts it, "Evil is contrary to nature; in fact it can only do harm to nature; and it would not be a fault to withdraw from God were it not that it is more natural to adhere to him. It is that fact which makes the withdrawal a fault. That is why the choice of evil is an impressive proof that the nature is good" (11.17).[7] It is not nature as such that is fallen in this account, but acts of the will, or "evil choices" that "make a wrong use of good natures" (11.17). This follows perfectly from the claim that evil is merely privative, that it has no positive, causative nature, that it is, as he puts it, "merely a name for the privation of good" (11.22). Furthermore, he is convinced that just because "sin has happened does not mean that the whole universe is full of sin, since by far the greater number of celestial beings preserve the order of their nature; and the evil will that refused to keep to the order of its nature did not for that reason escape the laws of God who orders all things well" (11.23). Rather, God founded "a Holy City constituted by the holy angels on high" that "receives its mode of being by subsisting in God, its enlightening by beholding him, its joy from cleaving to him. It exists; it sees; it loves. It is strong with God's eternity; it shines with God's truth; it rejoices in God's goodness" (11.24). And crucially, Augustine says that these holy angels, who are not on our arduous pilgrimage but who repose in the happiness of God's eternal rest, can help us without difficulty. The holy angels can help us even more easily than fallen angels can tempt us. That is because the holy angels have a power that is pure and free precisely because they participate in God's rest, and so they may help us, as it were, without effort, by the power of God's grace (11.31). Now this leads him to think about two societies of angels that are "contrasted and opposed," and not at all divorced from human affairs.

The contrasts should be predictable enough: one company enjoys God, the other swells with pride; one burns with holy love, the other "smoulders with the foul desire of its own exaltation"; one enjoys "the bright radiance of devotion," the other "rages in dark shadows of desire"; one brings merciful assistance in obedience to God, the other "seeths with the lust to subdue and to injure, at the behest of its own arrogance" (11.33). Importantly, Augustine stresses again that both societies are good by nature, but one is rightly directed by choice, while the other is perverted by choice. At the end of book 11, Augustine is thus satisfied to tell his readers, "so it seems

7. The tired analysis that the early Augustine was concerned with Manicheanism and the mature Augustine with Pelagianism falls to pieces in light of late texts like this one where it is clear that he affirms the goodness of human nature as such, and locates sin in the weakness of the will to adhere to God.

to me that we have sufficiently examined these two diverse and opposed communities of angels, *in which we find something like the beginnings of the two communities of mankind*" (11.34, emphasis mine). Bettenson's phrase "something like" is not in the original Latin. Augustine simply states that we find these two angelic societies at the origin of two human cities as well. And at the beginning of book 12, he is keen to reassert once again "that there is no absurdity or incongruity in asserting a fellowship between men and angels. So that there is no need to suppose four cities, two of angels and two of men" (12.1). There are only two cities, the difference between them rooted in their wills and desires, "the one sort persisting resolutely in that Good which is common to all [God himself, his eternity, love and truth] . . . while the others were delighted rather with their own power, as though they themselves were their own Good" (12.1).

4. The Pilgrim Church and the Two Cities

Now we must return to the basic two-cities narrative of Augustine, which is also Pauline. In Paul's letter to the Galatians he writes about Abraham's sons, one born of slavery, the other of freedom. The ekklesia is ontologically free, by virtue of baptism, to become children and citizens of the heavenly city. A pilgrim church drawing near to the heavenly city through her eucharistic devotion is an actual participation in the freedom of the heavenly city; it is a participation in the worship of God's holy angels who cry out the Trisagion, the Thrice Holy, sung without ceasing day and night, "Holy, holy, holy is God the Lord."[8] Augustine has no doubt that the Church has in its worship an actual share of this heavenly city now, communion not only with the saints who have been perfected in Christ, but also in communion with the holy angels who can assist in our perfection. As Erik Peterson put it, the sacramental "acts of the Church . . . [and] all earthly worship by the Church would be understood as participation in the worship that the angels offer to God in heaven."[9] There is a link between the earthly and heavenly liturgies, and it is of course a eucharistic bond that elevates the Church's hymnody far above the hymnody of the nations. And here we can begin to see the political, or rather *supra-political*, nature of the way in which God has established, as Augustine puts it in *City* 17.4, a new polis

---

8. Erik Peterson, *Theological Tractates*, ed. and trans. Michael J. Hollerich (Stanford: Stanford University Press, 2011) 110.

9. Ibid., 108.

whose king and founder is Christ. The blood of the Lamb has created a new people who sing a new transcendent song, a song that transcends the nations, the ethnos, the folk, the national, the local, by participating in the praise of the eternal worship of the angels and the blessed, the citizens of the heavenly city.

For Augustine, the Church is pilgrim. As he puts it in his *Explanations of the Psalms*, "This Church begins from Jerusalem, the earthly one, that she may then rejoice in God in that other Jerusalem which is heavenly: it begins from the one, it ends in the other."[10] Of course, the Church and the City of God are not coterminous for Augustine, but they are strongly associated in the very idea of the pilgrim church, whose mystical, heavenly reality is inscribed on her very origin, mission, and destiny. Moreover, the cultic acts of the *ecclesia catholica* are also understood as super-political acts, ordered to the transcendent Jerusalem, and assisted by those already resident there, namely, the angels and saints. From these acts, the powers and principalities flee from the witness of our obedience to Christ. The nations may flee as well, but they will only do so to the extent that their gods are unclean spirits. The clarion call of Augustine's *City of God* is not, however, about a Church that will rule, but about a humanity liberated from these self-destructive arrogant powers and principalities, and free for eternal happiness in the worship of the one true God, to be made partakers of God's own nature, and to participate in the celestial worship, on the side of the angels and saints.

---

10. Augustine, *En. in ps.* 147, PL 37:1929; quoted in ibid., 234 n. 3.

6

Christ and the Free Market

Daniel M. Bell Jr.

A FEW WEEKS INTO an ethics course I teach, I ask the class to consider the baptismal liturgy. Specifically we look at the renunciations: "Do you renounce all the forces of evil . . . ?"[1] "Do you renounce the spiritual forces of wickedness, reject the evil powers of this world . . . ?"[2] Then I ask the class to imagine they are duly called and appointed church leaders, facing a catechumen who asks, "What am I getting myself into? This sounds like an exorcism. Who or what are these powers?" I press the question, asking them not to dodge it with vague abstractions but to get specific, concrete. Name the Powers. The typical response is puzzled silence.

Why do we have such a hard time naming the powers? In his important work on the topic, Hendrik Berkhof considers the invisibility of the powers and principalities and suggests, "the capacity to recognize [the Powers as described by] the Apostle Paul has to do with the way in which the reader experiences and understands *his own culture*. There are many times and regions where these texts remain a sealed book. And then

---

1. Evangelical Lutheran Church in America, *Lutheran Book of Worship*, baptismal liturgy, §10 (123).
2. The United Methodist Church, *The United Methodist Hymnal*, baptismal liturgy I, §4 (34).

suddenly conditions can arise which make it visible that these words have a power to unveil and liberate."[3]

Many scholars attribute the difficulty of engaging the Powers to ancient cosmology. Simply put, moderns find talk of powers and principalities incredible, a species of superstition, a reflection of an antiquated mythology.

My sense is that this does not quite hit the mark. The stumbling block is not fundamentally a matter of cosmology but of control. The problem is not so much angels as agency. We think we are, or at least we aspire to be, in control. Autonomy, independence are hallmarks of our age and our anthropology.

Accordingly, when we think about baptism—if we think about baptism—we imagine the renunciations directed at things over which we can exercise control. Sin becomes a personal matter. It is basically a failure of my will, of my self-control and what I am doing in baptism is committing to exercise better control, to muster the willpower to set aside my personal peccadillos.[4]

Of course, a straightforward reading of the liturgy does not support such an understanding of baptism, and when the liturgy is reconnected with the tradition and the biblical, and especially Pauline, corpus, it is clearly reductionistic.

Indeed, one of the rather fascinating aspects of baptism is precisely that we renounce things over which we really have no control. In this sense, baptism is clear: we are in bondage. We are held captive by sin. In the waters of baptism we find ourselves tossed into the middle of something greater than our personal struggles with our own peccadillos. We find ourselves caught up in a cosmic drama, beholden to powers that exceed our feeble, easily distracted wills.

And this is what the Pauline discourse on powers and principalities is all about: control, dominion, and who has it. And the answer is, disturbingly perhaps, not us. Which is why it is so appropriate to talk about economy, and specifically capitalism or the free market economy, as a power or principality.[5] The free market exercises a dominion over our lives that clearly exceeds the ability of our power to change.

---

3. Hendrik Berkhof, *Christ and the Powers*, trans. John Howard Yoder (Scottdale, PA: Herald, 1977) 11. Emphasis added.

4. This comment is not meant to deny that God acts in baptism or the primacy of God's act. I am only suggesting that insofar as baptism does entail a human response, that response is framed in terms of my agency.

5. Following Berkhof, *Christ and the Powers*, 14, and Walter Wink, *Naming the*

As Berkhof suggested, sometimes conditions can arise that make visible that which was invisible, intelligible that which was unintelligible, and credible that which was incredible. In the wake of the collapse of the Soviet Union—and with it, the mistaken hopes for Marxism as a path to paradise—the noted Christian apologist for the current economic order, Michael Novak, gleefully announced, "We are all capitalist now."[6] And we celebrated for almost two decades, while the bubble was being inflated.

Then suddenly we found ourselves on the brink of disaster in a global market dominated by corporate persons too big to fail, a market hell-bent on becoming a total market, subordinating everything—everyone, every space—to a capitalist logic. The result: the complete marketization of society, where anything and everything has a price and is for sale; where we are encouraged to calculate relationships—like marriage—according to a marginalist logic of cost and benefit; where children are viewed as consumer goods and fashion accessories, and schools are factories for the manufacture of workers and consumers; and where the old and ill are lambasted as Greedy Geezers who dare to live their unproductive lives too long instead of quietly checking out, perhaps adrift on an ice flow melting in our warming and increasingly toxic seas.

We find ourselves in the midst of a market that seeks freedom, no limits, and that is too big to fail. This free market is too big to fail not only in the sense that its dominion is so extensive that were it to fail, surely chaos would swallow us, but in another sense as well: after Marxism, we cannot imagine an alternative. The free market increasingly dominates not only our lives but our imaginations as well, so much so that some have linked it with the end of history.[7] It is a tremendous Power indeed.

In what follows I will unpack capitalism as a power in more detail, considering what it does to us and what is wrong with it. Then I take up the question of alternatives, raising the issue of Christ and the powers. What is Christ doing here and now to set us free from the Power of the free market?

Powers (Philadelphia: Fortress, 1984) 9–10, I use the terms interchangeably.

6. Michael Novak, *The Catholic Ethic and the Spirit of Capitalism* (New York: Free Press, 1993) 101.

7. Francis Fukuyama, "The End of History?," *The National Interest* 16 (1989) 3–18. See also Francis Fukuyama, *The End of History and the Last Man* (New York: Free Press, 2006).

The Power of the Free Market: What Work Does It Do?[8]

The Powers and Principalities are associated with a host of supra-human forces that influence human life and society. They exercise dominion and so order and structure human existence. Accordingly, we might ask, how does the free market order human life?

The answer, of course, depends on who you ask. Some people argue that capitalism is an amazing economic order that has lifted many people out of poverty and holds the potential to raise up the still languishing masses. Others argue that capitalism exacerbates the plight of the poor as it aids the rich in their exploitation of the poor.

In other words, evaluating or assessing the free market typically hinges upon answering the question, does it work? Does it help impoverished people escape poverty or does it perpetuate their plight?

The empirical focus is good and appropriate insofar as it reflects a near-consensus among Christians that concern for persons who are poor is a proper task of an economic order and therefore is an important measure of the morality of an economy.

However, the question whether it works is the wrong question to put to capitalism. It is the wrong question because, quite frankly, it is rather obvious that capitalism does in fact work. No economic order has so obviously displayed such an enormous productive capacity. Accordingly, a better, more accurate question would be, *what* work does it do?

Capitalism and Desire

What work does capitalism do? Peter Berger, another noted Christian defender of capitalism, has asserted, "From its inception, capitalism has been a force of cataclysmic transformation in one country after another. Capitalism has radically changed every material, social, political, and cultural facet of the societies it has touched, and it continues to do so. Understanding this revolutionary impact of capitalism . . . is a formidable and important intellectual task."[9]

---

8. This essay is an introduction to several themes and issues I develop much more substantially in *The Economy of Desire: Christianity and Capitalism in a Postmodern World* (Grand Rapid: Baker Academic, 2012).

9. Peter Berger, *The Capitalist Revolution: Fifty Propositions about Prosperity, Equality, and Liberty* (New York: Basic Books, 1986) 3.

When we think about economy, we often think in terms of the allocation, production and distribution of material goods and services. Likewise, capitalism is often thought of in terms of a mode of production, associated with the confluence of capital and abstract labor. Perhaps there was a time when the market economy could be conceived as constrained, limited, just one small part of life alongside other dimensions of life like culture, politics, civic life and religion.[10] But not anymore.

As Berger noted, capitalism is a cataclysmic force that effects radical changes not just in the economic order of things but in every register of life—social, cultural, political. The habits we learn in the market, the "economic way of human behavior,"[11] are not confined to the market but increasingly inform and shape our behavior in all aspects of life. I mentioned several examples at the outset of this essay, dealing with marriage and children, schools, caring for the ill and the elderly. But there are many others. Consider the widespread influence of market behavior on how we think about the mission of the church. Think of the normalcy of church shopping, pastors presenting themselves as CEOs, and how Jesus and religion are presented in ways that mimic consumer marketing.[12] Or recall the words of the president after 9/11 encouraging us to shop. (This is *not* a criticism of an individual; rather, it is merely indicative of the power of the free market to form and shape our politics.) The free market's dominion reaches far beyond narrowly or traditionally economic matters.

As that dominion has expanded, as the market has become "freer," it has become easier to see that capitalism is a way of life (often called "consumerism"), a cultural logic, a system of formation, a discipline. It molds us, our behavior. It shapes our identity. Capitalism forms particular kinds of persons and particular kinds of communities. It encourages some practices and habits and precludes or prevents others.

It is a principality or power that forms and shapes the constitutive power of life—our desire, or we could say, our loves. It disciplines our desire. I was created to desire God, yet I do not want to go to church; I want to go shopping. I am called to love my neighbors as myself; yet I find myself competing with them for the means to sustain life and flourish. Though the

10. See Karl Polanyi, *The Great Transformation* (Boston: Beacon, 1971).

11. See Gary S. Becker, *The Economic Approach to Human Behavior* (Chicago: University of Chicago Press, 1976).

12. See Philp D. Kenneson and James L. Street, *Selling Out the Church: The Dangers of Church Marketing* (Nashville: Abingdon, 1997); Michael Budde, *The (Magic) Kingdom of God: Christianity and the Global Culture Industries* (Boulder, CO: Westview, 1998).

Lord is my shepherd and I shall not want, it seems to me that I never—and never can—have enough.

Christians frequently lament the "materialism" that seems to drive the economy; many a preacher has waxed prophetic on the evils of materialism. The materialism charge, however, misses the mark when it comes to capitalism. As its Christian proponents rightly point out, capitalism is not crassly materialistic but rather is deeply attuned to the human spirit, to the desires of the human heart.

That capitalism is fundamentally about desire is evident in several of the classic definitions of economics. Consider this one, offered by Lionel Robbins: "Economics is the science which studies human behavior as a relationship between ends and scarce means which have alternative uses."[13] The reference to scarcity is often taken to refer to the material limits of a finite world, but it is actually a statement about human desire. Another common definition makes this clearer when it notes that economics is "the social science that deals with the ways in which men [sic] and societies seek to satisfy their material needs and desires."[14] The free market economy is powered by human desire; it depends on, even requires human desire to exceed material production. If it were truly materialistic, the market for smartphones would have collapsed after everyone had one.

Capitalism and Communion

The first part of the answer to the question of how the power that is the free market orders human life is that it disciplines desire. In some sense, this is obvious and so constitutes rather low-hanging fruit. Notwithstanding the boilerplate denials of Madison Avenue, recognition that the market seeks to manufacture and manipulate desire is widespread.

The second part of the answer expands upon this claim in less obvious ways. In order to do this, however, I will begin with a seemingly unrelated question: What are people for? Why are we here?

The psalmist writes, "As a deer longs for flowing streams, so my soul longs for you, O God" (Ps 42:1). Augustine echoed this when he famously asserted that our hearts are restless until they rest in God. Thomas Aquinas

---

13. Lionel Robbins, *An Essay on the Nature and Significance of Economic Science* (London: Macmillan, 1952) 16. Emphasis added.

14. Albert Rees, cited in Becker, *Economic Approach*, 3. See also Edwin Mansfield, *Principles of Macroeconomics*, 7th ed. (New York: Norton, 1992) 5.

made the same point a bit differently when he said that our end is beatitude, blessedness, which is nothing less than friendship with God. And the Calvinist divines who met at Westminster in 1647 made a similar claim when they declared that the chief end of the human being is to worship and enjoy God. In other words, people are for desiring, delighting in God and reflecting God's glory. We are created for friendship, for communion, with God.

Of course, this friendship is not merely a matter of me and God, of me and Jesus. After all, Scripture reminds us that we cannot be friends of God if we hate our neighbors (1 John 3:17; 4:20–21) and that redemption involves breaking down the walls of hostility that divide peoples (Eph 2; Gal 3:28); hence, the commandments are succinctly summed up in the exhortation that we "love God and neighbor" (Matt 22:35–40).

What, then, is the problem? If we were created to desire God and live in communion with one another in God, why are our hearts so clearly not at rest? If we are created for friendship, why do we have to pray for our enemies? Why do we live in fear of our neighbors and constantly look over our shoulder at the stranger? The Christian tradition accounts for this in terms of sin.

What is sin at its heart? Not merely breaking the rules or doing what we should not, although a full account of sin would certainly encompass those. Recalling both Augustine and the Calvinist divines, we might construe sin as fundamentally a matter of the corruption of our desire. We were created to desire God and the things of God, to delight in and enjoy God and to revel in God's glory; yet, in sin we no longer do so. We do not desire God and the things of God. Our desire is disordered. As the prophet Isaiah suggests (55:1), we desire things that do not satisfy. It would not be too strong to say that we are enslaved, held captive, by this disordered desire (cf. 1 Tim 6:9). That is why our hearts are restless.

Furthermore, recalling Aquinas as well as Scripture, we might elaborate a bit more and describe sin in terms of a breach or rupture of communion. We were created for friendship with God and one another, yet captive to our disordered desires we struggle, fight, compete (cf. Jas 4:1–3; Gen 4–11). As the early church taught, sin is a matter of division, of the breach or rupture of communion. For this reason, Origen declared that where there is sin, there is a multitude, and Maximus the Confessor observed that our post-fall condition is such that "now we rend each other like wild beasts."[15] Unfortunately, far too often this is a painfully accurate description of what we see displayed in the headlines day after day.

What does any of this have to do with the free market economy? As suggested previously, capitalism is a discipline of desire. It has everything to do with how life, desire, our loves are ordered and organized toward particular ends and purposes. More specifically, the question what are people for has everything to do with capitalism because capitalism embodies a very different answer to the question than the classic Christian tradition. Put a bit more pointedly, the capitalist economy of desire is a manifestation of sin because it corrupts desire and so obstructs communion. Capitalism is wrong because it distorts human desire, so that it no longer flows according to its proper, created end; it twists desire and in so doing obstructs our friendship with God, one another, and creation. The problem with capitalism is that it does not facilitate but instead actively works against the divine will for the renewal of communion with God and humanity.

In this regard, consider how capitalism forms and shapes human desire and so human relations with one another and with God. Consider first capitalism's production of the human being, the vaunted *Homo economicus*. This is the self-made, autonomous individual who is afflicted by an unquenchable and insatiable desire that results in its being driven to maximize its interests and chafe against anything that would impinge upon its freedom to choose.

Given the character of the human so constructed, it is unsurprising that under capitalism human relations are characterized by competition, struggle, conflict. In the absence of a common good, individuals are left to struggle to secure private goods and interests against other individuals, who must now be viewed as a threat. All of us, winners and losers, First World consumers and Fourth World excluded, compete for resources, for market share, for a living wage, for a job, for the time for friendship and family, for inclusion in the market, and so forth. Furthermore, as already suggested, everything and everyone increasingly is treated like a commodity and subject to the cost-benefit logic of efficiency.

Accordingly, relations become instrumental and contractual as others are viewed in terms of how they serve or hinder our self-interested pursuits. In the worst case, we learn to view others as mere commodities, bodies to be exploited, consumed, discarded. Think of slavery, organ-mining, or the

---

15. Cited in Henri de Lubac, *Catholicism*, trans. Lancelot C. Sheppard and Elizabeth Englund (San Francisco: Ignatius, 1988) 33–34.

sex trade. The free market shapes life as a Darwinian struggle where the highly productive and profitable are valued, while the less productive and marketable are disposable.

Where is God in all this, and how do humanity and divinity relate? What does the capitalist order of things imply about God's way with the world? One of the best-known features of the free market economy is the so-called invisible hand. The invisible hand of the market is a kind of surrogate for divine providence that functions almost sacramentally, transforming the individual pursuit of self-interest into the good of the whole. To echo an early critic of the capitalist order, the invisible hand takes private vice and turns it into public virtue.

What is particularly striking about this account is what it does *not* say about God. God is not active now redeeming humanity from sin. Sin is an ineradicable given[16] and for the time being at least, we are inescapably interest maximizers. The most that can be said about God and sin now is that sin is being managed through the mechanism of the market. (This is a very Deistic or Stoic conception of God.)

The leading Christian proponents of capitalism are clear on this point. The kingdom of God is not of this world and therefore prior to Jesus's return in final victory we cannot expect to order or live our economic lives in any other way. In this time between the times, the kingdom is at best an invisible reality that encompasses the hearts of individuals in their vertical relation with God. The love revealed in the Gospel does not order or transform life in the rough and tumble of this world.[17] Said a little differently, God might justify sinners now but God is not sanctifying them now.

But this is not all. The god of capitalism is a god who did not create enough. Scarcity, God's failure to provide enough, is the starting point for the free market economy. God's afflicting creation with scarcity is the beginning of the commercial war that is capitalism. Indeed, it is scarcity that primes the creative, entrepreneurial pump that drives us into the market. In this way, God is cast as a kind of sadistic cosmic Easter bunny, hiding stuff from humanity so that in the conflict and competition to create and produce, individuals will develop various traits and capacities.

---

16. Michael Novak, *The Spirit of Democratic Capitalism* (New York: Simon and Schuster, 1982) 82.

17. Robert Benne, *The Paradoxical Vision: A Public Theology for the Twenty-First Century* (Minneapolis: Fortress, 1995) 86–87.

Redeeming the Power That Is Economy: What Is God Doing Now?

When I suggested that capitalism was best approached as a discipline of desire, I acknowledged that in some sense such a claim is rather low-hanging fruit. The capitalist manipulation of desire is obvious. Well, the same could be said about the theological critique I just advanced. It too is low-hanging fruit in the sense that few Christian advocates of capitalism would deny that capitalism is not the kingdom. Michael Novak is not atypical in this regard when he writes, "Capitalism itself is not even close to being the kingdom of God.... The presuppositions, ethos, moral habits, and way of life required for the smooth functioning of democratic and capitalist institutions are not a full expression of Christian or Jewish faith, and are indeed partially in conflict with the full transcendent demands of Christian and Jewish faith."[18] Capitalism's Christian defenders do not presume capitalism is perfect.

What they argue is that capitalism is realistic. It does not assume that human beings are saints and angels. Rather, in the words of one economist, capitalism is lauded as a system under which "bad men can do least harm."[19] It is a system that "does not depend for its functioning on our finding good men for running it, or on all men becoming better than they are now."[20] Indeed, it is thought to be a virtue of capitalism that it reduces the need for compassion, fraternal love, and solidarity.[21] As Dennis Robertson famously noted, if economists assist in rightly arranging the economic order, they can "contribute mightily to the economizing ... of that scarce resource Love."[22]

Thus, the moral and theological debate over capitalism revolves around whether a better alternative is possible here and now. It is an argument over whether Christ is dethroning and redeeming the Powers now.

---

18. Novak, *Spirit of Capitalism*, 227–28.

19. Friedrich A. Hayek, *Individualism and Economic Order* (Chicago: University of Chicago Press, 1948) 11.

20. Ibid., 12.

21. Robert Benne, *The Ethic of Democratic Capitalism: A Moral Reassessment* (Philadelphia: Fortress, 1981) 143; see also 154. Herman E. Daly and John B. Cobb Jr. make this observation as well in their book *For the Common Good*, 2nd ed. (Boston: Beacon, 1994) 50–51, 89, 92.

22. Dennis H. Robertson, *Economic Commentaries* (Westport, CT: Greenwood, 1978) 152, 154.

Christian proponents of capitalism argue that, given the alternatives, capitalism is the best we can do.

Here we get to the heart of the matter. Capitalism is said to be the best we can do, *given* the alternatives. Well, what are we given? What does God give here and now? What is God doing here and now about sin? When we read in Colossians that God in Christ disarmed the powers and principalities and made a public example of them, what does that mean? What does it mean to renounce the powers and principalities in baptism? What is God doing here and now to heal our disordered desire? Is God simply managing sin? Are we stuck looking forward to the arrival of a savior who at some point in the future will free us from our capitalist captivity? What is the alternative to capitalism?

From a Christian point of view, the alternative is rather straightforward. The alternative to capitalism is the divine economy, the kingdom of God, where those who build, inhabit; where those who plant, harvest; where all are filled and every thirst is slaked from the bounty of the Lord's table. It is a gift economy where material goods circulate in accord with what John Paul II calls their "universal destination,"[23] that is, it is an economy where the production and distribution of material goods nurtures the communion of all in the common good that is God.

Is such a divine economy possible now? Christian proponents of capitalism say no.[24] Whatever effect the kingdom has now, it does not make possible an alternative to capitalism. As previously noted, Christian defenses of capitalism rest on the claim that God is not redeeming us from sin here and now and so the best, most realistic thing we can expect in the present age is that sin can be managed by the market.[25]

---

23. John Paul II, *Centesimus Annus*, paras. 30–31

24. See, for instance, Michael Novak, "God and Man in the Corporation," *Policy Review* 3 (1980) 27.

25. Indeed, at their most extreme, the conviction that sin is inescapably part of our economic life is not limited to the assertion that it is inescapable in this time before Christ returns. Rather, it becomes a claim that we will never be free of sin. Thus writes Novak, "The point of the Incarnation is to respect the world as it is . . . and to disbelieve any promises that the world is now or ever will be transformed into the City of God. . . . The world is not going to become—ever—a kingdom of justice and love. . . . The single greatest temptation for Christians is to imagine that the salvation won by Jesus has altered the human condition." He goes on to write, "The future may not have an upward slant, except as Golgotha had: So be it." Novak, *Spirit of Democratic Capitalism*, 341–43; 73.

Put in traditional theological terms, Christian defenses of capitalism release the tension between the "already" and "not yet" that characterizes Christian life. We confess that the kingdom has *already* appeared in Christ, and is a reality even now, even if it has *not yet* appeared in its fullness or completion. As Paul says, we are the ones on whom the ends of the ages have come (1 Cor 10:11). The baptized live the life of the kingdom now, even in the midst of, overlapping with, the passing old age (1 Cor 7:31) of the Powers and Principalities.[26]

Thus, baptism marks a transfer of allegiance, a passing from one dominion or lord to another. As N. T. Wright puts it, the Christian life is "the summons to live in God's new world, on the basis that idolatry and sin *have been defeated* at the cross and new creation *has begun* at Easter—and that the entire new world, based on this achievement, is guaranteed by the power of the Spirit."[27]

Christian proponents of capitalism inevitably release this tension by emptying the "already" of any immediate material (social-political-economic) content, with the result that we are left with the capitalist status quo as the lesser evil, as the best we can expect until at some future point God decides to redeem us.

But the Good News is that we are not alone, left to enduring sin's management, while waiting for God to act in the future. At the heart of the Christian faith is the confession that in Christ the kingdom has come near (Matt 4:17). In Christ, the powers have been dethroned—which means that God's economy is a real, genuine possibility even here and now.

Where Is the Divine Economy?

Where is this divine economy? Where is the proof that Christ has disarmed the powers and principalities and made an example of them? In Ephesians Paul writes, "through the church the wisdom of God . . . might now be made known to the rulers and authorities in the heavenly places" (3:10). Through

---

26. This is not to deny that, in Luther's memorable words, the old Adam is a good swimmer, that is, that Christians continue to wrestle with the remains of sin in this life, whether due to our being "double beings" or because the Powers do not relinquish authority without a fight, thus rendering the way of Christ the way of the cross. The point is, to use classic theological language, baptism marks the end of sin's reign, even if sin remains while we are sanctified.

27. N. T. Wright, *Evil and the Justice of God* (Downers Grove, IL: InterVarsity, 2006) 120; emphasis added.

the Spirit God gathers persons together into a body (Christ's body) called church where, by means of the divine things in our midst—Word and sacrament, catechesis, orders, and discipline—human desire is being healed of its capitalist distortions and set free to share in and witness to a different economic ordering where material goods are produced and circulate for the sake of extending communion.

In more recognizably political and economic terms, this divine economy takes the form of what the Christian tradition calls the works of mercy. The works of mercy name the in-breaking of God's economy, the beginning of the redemption of the Power that is economy and the reordering of human desire and society in line with God's reign. Although they do not explicitly address every dimension of the divine economy, they are nevertheless a good starting point for outlining the practices that constitute that economy in everyday life.

As they developed and were formally specified, the works of mercy embraced seven corporeal (bodily) and seven spiritual works. According to Aquinas, they are as follows:[28]

Corporal works	*Spiritual works*
• feed the hungry	• instruct the ignorant
• give drink to the thirsty	• counsel the doubtful
• clothe the naked	• comfort the mourning
• shelter the homeless	• reprove the sinner
• visit the sick	• forgive injuries
• ransom the captive (minister to prisoners)	• bear wrongs patiently
• bury the dead	• pray for all

The works of mercy were at the heart of what has been called "the Christian revolution," the profound change that the birth and spread of Christianity effected in the Roman world and beyond. Whereas the practice of beneficence was not foreign to ancient Roman and Greek cultures, it was specifically directed toward the city and citizens.[29] Furthermore, the precepts of classical morality considered mercy and unearned aid to be immoral and unjust.[30] Into this world came the good news of a merciful God

---

28. Aquinas, *Summa Theologica*, II-II 32.2.

29. Peter Brown, *Poverty and Leadership in the Later Roman Empire* (Hanover, NH: University Press of New England, 2002) 4–5.

30. Rodney Stark, *The Rise of Christianity* (San Francisco: HarperCollins, 1997) 212. Edwin A. Judge, "The Quest for Mercy in Late Antiquity," in *God Who Is Rich in Mercy*, ed. Peter T. O'Brien and David G. Peterson (Grand Rapids: Baker, 1986) 107.

whose followers were about the work of extending this mercy beyond their own, beyond family, tribe and city, to include the stranger and persons who are poor.[31]

As the church spread and developed, the works of mercy took shape in a host of charitable institutions and practices that encompassed laity, religious orders, and church leaders.[32] Bishops had a special responsibility to care for the poor in their jurisdiction and they did so by founding shelters and providing food. Hostels, hospices, and hospitals were founded by the church and laity for the sake of sheltering the poor, the traveler, the sick. Nursing, the idea that one would care for instead of abandon the gravely ill, was a Christian invention.[33] Homes for children, orphans, lepers, ex-prostitutes, the elderly, widows, and mentally ill were established. Schools were erected for the poor; legal aid was provided them as well. Professional, civic and religious groups (orders, fraternities, guilds) were formed for the sake of establishing and sustaining such institutions and practices, for ransoming captives, for paying the dowries of poor women, and for supporting public works such as roads and bridges. In sum, in ways and to an extent that are difficult to imagine today, given both the capitalist deformity of desire as well as modernity's self-justifying caricaturing of the church before modernity, the works of mercy permeated Christian society.[34]

The extent and effect of the works of mercy were such that the pagan emperor Julian complained in 362 CE that the withering of the pagan faith was connected to Christianity's benevolence to strangers and care for persons who are poor, even pagan poor.[35] This calls to mind, as well, Adam Smith's lamentation in *The Wealth of Nations* that it was the church's prac-

---

31. Christianity followed Judaism in this regard. See Ramsay MacMullen, *Christianizing the Roman Empire (A.D. 100–400)* (New Haven: Yale University Press, 1984) 54.

32. See James F. Keenan, *The Works of Mercy* (Lanham, MD: Rowman & Littlefield, 2005); James W. Broadman, *Charity and Welfare: Hospitals and the Poor in Medieval Catalonia* (Philadelphia: University of Pennsylvania Press, 1998); James W. Broadman, *Charity and Religion in Medieval Europe* (Washington DC: Catholic University of America Press, 2009); John Henderson, *Piety and Charity in Late Medieval Florence* (Chicago: University of Chicago Press, 1994); Antony Black, *Guild and State* (New Brunswick, NJ: Transaction Publishers, 2003); Michel Mollat, *The Poor in the Middle Ages*, trans. Arthur Goldhammer (New Haven: Yale University Press, 1986); Brian Tierney, *Medieval Poor Law* (Berkeley: University of California Press, 1959).

33. See Stark, *Rise of Christianity*, 73–94.

34. This account is not meant to deny the failures and abuses that mar the Christian tradition.

35. Stark, *Rise of Christianity*, 84.

tice of the works of mercy that posed the greatest obstacle to the emergence of the free market. He goes on to rejoice that the economy was eventually able to break the back of the church, rendering its charity more sparse, thereby undercutting its spiritual and temporal authority.[36]

It must be admitted that recognizing the works of mercy as an economic alternative to the free market is difficult, and it is so for several reasons. First, under the sign of modernity, the works of mercy have been reduced from a way of life that engages the allocation, production, and distribution of material goods to "extra-economic" practices like private philanthropy and government welfare.

Yet, rightly understood and practiced the works of mercy are not private. They characterize the public life of those who have switched allegiances from the Powers to God's rule, Christ's lordship, in all that they do. The works are an instantiation of what Luther calls the freedom of a Christian, that condition whereby our whole life becomes a surplus to be given away in labor and service to our neighbors.[37] Accordingly, the works of mercy are not synonymous with what Christians may do for an hour or two during their spare time—volunteering at a food bank or shelter, for example.

It follows that the works of mercy are neither optional nor voluntary. Rather, they are at the heart of our mission and ministry to extend communion in Christ. In a powerful passage, Augustine makes exactly this point, noting how participation in Communion shapes our desire to serve and extend community. The soul offered to God, he observes, is inflamed by the fire of God's love, receives God's beauty and is remolded in the image of permanent loveliness. As the church celebrates the sacrifice of Christ at the altar in communion, it is joined to that sacrifice and so receives the form of a servant. It then goes forth to make true sacrifices, which, Augustine says, are works of mercy that relieve distress and draw persons into communion with God.[38]

Nor are the works of mercy "extra-economic" in the sense of only addressing market failures, providing a safety net for those who lose the capitalist competition. This is a major shortcoming of both philanthropy

---

36. Adam Smith, *An Inquiry into the Nature and Causes of the Wealth of Nations*, ed. Edwin Cannan (Chicago: University of Chicago Press, 1976), bk. 5, ch. 1, pt. 3, art. 3.

37. Martin Luther, "The Freedom of a Christian," in vol. 31 of *Luther's Works*, ed. Harold J. Grimm (Philadelphia: Muhlenberg, 1957) 364–68.

38. Augustine, *City of God* 10.6.

and welfare. They do not challenge unjust systems; they only pick up after them. Furthermore, those practices do not have as their goal the extension of communion. Philanthropy may meet material needs but does not nurture communion; welfare attempts to reinsert people into the market.

In contrast, the works of mercy name a social, political, economic way of life that challenges injustice by offering an alternative way of life that counters the free market by using material goods for the sake of extending communion. With a little reflection, it is not difficult to see how the works of mercy address not only distribution but also production, not only individuals but also systems, not only material needs but also relational needs for communion. Recall the history of the works of mercy previously cited. They constituted a political economy, a civil economy that unites charity and economy, gift and contract, virtue and the market.[39]

Conclusion: What Do You See?

There is another reason it is difficult to recognize the works of mercy as the in-breaking of the divine economy. If, as Berkhof suggested, the Powers can be hard to see, so too can God's dethroning and redemption of the Powers.

Part of the difficulty is that when we think of an alternative economic order, we look for the wrong thing. We tend to look for a full-blown economy, a kind of Christian trade zone or economic block, separate and distinct from worldly economic orders, perhaps accompanied by its own treatise like *The Wealth of Nations* or Mankiw's *Principles of Economics*.

But, alas, our calling is not to withdraw from the world and establish our own economic colony somewhere. Rather, just as Jeremiah encouraged our Jewish elders to embrace their scattering (diaspora) as an opportunity to witness and just as Augustine reminded the early Christians that the City of God is deliberately intermingled with the cities of this world, we are called to live out the divine economy in the midst of the capitalist order for the sake of witnessing to God's redemption of the powers and principalities. We are called to be an example that makes known to the Powers and Principalities that Christ is Lord and they are not, that provides the world an example of a redeemed economy that does not dominate but rather serves communion.

---

39. See Luigino Bruni and Stefano Zamagni, *Civil Economy: Efficiency, Equity, Public Happiness* (New York: P. Lang, 2007) 30; see also chapters 2–4.

Yet, even if we change our perspective and embrace the divine economy as a diaspora or pilgrim movement amidst the world's economies, the suspicion may yet linger that escape from capitalism is not possible, that the capitalist discipline of desire is too effective, its hold on our desires too deep and all-pervasive.

In the Gospel of Matthew, the disciples of John confront Jesus with the question of whether he is the long-awaited Messiah. Jesus responds to the skeptics of his day by pointing out what they see and hear: the blind see, the lame walk, the lepers are cleansed, the deaf hear, the dead are raised, and the poor have the good news brought to them (Matt 11:2–5).

So we might ask with regard to the divine economy on pilgrimage in this world, what do we see? Are the works of mercy being embodied in the midst of the capitalist order as an alternative to that order? Is desire being healed of its capitalist distortions?

The answer is yes, if we have eyes to see, if we have eyes not simply for the kingdom in its fullness but rather for glimpses of the divine economy on pilgrimage in this time between the times. If we have eyes to see, then all around us, in the midst of the economies of this world, the divine economy appears in a variety of practices and forms challenging the capitalist order of things and freeing desire to flow in the joyous conviviality of love. In a manner not unlike the medieval works of mercy, today the divine economy appears in our midst in an array of institutions and practices that encompass lay and ordained, congregations and intentional communities, as well as institutions and initiatives organized by both church leaders and laity.

We can catch glimpses of the divine economy present here and now, in the midst of this world, in the practices of simplicity and solidarity. Exploring the discipline of simplicity, Christians are resisting the consumerist culture of capitalism and reordering their lives in accord with the common good and the universal destination of material goods. In the practice of solidarity, Christians are exercising hospitality, sanctuary, and—in efforts like the Jubilee campaign—calling for the restructuring of the global economy. They are using the division of labor and alternative markets as opportunities to pursue and establish just relations, fair trade, with persons around the globe as they reconnect the goods and services they use with the conditions of their production and distribution.

Congregations and intentional Christian communities, like the Catholic Worker movement, the New Monasticism, Focolare, and others, likewise are embodying the divine economy as they establish small groups for the sake of strengthening economic discipleship by means of accountability and support. They are developing alternative markets, such as Seeds of Hope and Church Supported Agriculture, and supporting fair trade in an increasing array of products. They are moving beyond philanthropy and the handout in an effort to develop community.[40]

The divine economy is also being revealed in more traditional business enterprises such as the Economy of Communion initiative and the Mondragon Cooperative Corporation, both of which are shaped by the Christian economy of desire.

Although they are not widely recognized and lauded, the divine economy is active in these and a multitude of other efforts like them, from conversations beginning in congregations regarding the nature of "enough," what money cannot buy, what constitutes a just or living wage, the nature of corporate social responsibility, the traditional ban on usury, and so forth. In all these ways and many more, God is present here and now dethroning the free market, healing desire of its disorder, circulating material gifts, like bread and wine, to inflame our hearts and remold our desire in the image of permanent loveliness for the sake of the renewal of the communion for which we were all created.

---

40. See, for example, Alan and Debra Hirsch, *Untamed: Reactivating a Missional Form of Discipleship* (Grand Rapids: Baker, 2010); John Perkins, *Beyond Charity: The Call to Christian Community Development* (Grand Rapids: Baker, 1993); Alan Roxburgh and Fred Romanuk, *The Missional Leader: Equipping Your Church to Reach a Changing World* (San Francisco: Jossey-Bass, 2006).

7

Technology as Principality
The Elimination of Incarnation

P. Travis Kroeker

IN AN EASTER OP-ED in the *New York Times*,[1] Simon Critchley (Hans Jonas Professor of Philosophy at the New School for Social Research) makes an equation between the Christian hope of the resurrection and Prometheus the Titan, who stole fire from the gods and gave it as a gift to human beings. In Aeschylus' version, not only is Prometheus thus responsible for the gift to humans of "technology" (all the arts of progressive human civilization); he is also responsible for a second, more "spiritual" gift: "I stopped mortals from foreseeing doom," says Prometheus. "I sowed in them blind hopes." According to Critchley, the Apostle Paul inadvertently confirms this second Promethean gift in asserting that the Christian hope in resurrection is precisely a blind hope: "Now hope that is seen is not hope. For who hopes for what he sees?" (Rom 8:24; cf. Heb 11:1). The problem, Critchley implies, is that when blind hope of a spiritual kind is tied to civilizational arts and especially political ideals, we are in danger of being deluded by the

---

1. Simon Critchley, "Abandon (Nearly) All Hope," *New York Times*, April 19, 2014, http://opinionator.blogs.nytimes.com/2014/04/19/abandon-nearly-all-hope/?_r=0.

most blatant and painful forms of unreality that prolong human bondage and suffering.

In this regard, of course, Critchley is in agreement with Nietzsche's scathing critique of Paul's spiritual causality, which he considers to be "completely out of touch with reality."[2] The belief in resurrection puts the scandal of miracle at the very heart of reality: God creates the world *ex nihilo* at each moment: the world is not an immanent becoming according to causal laws of nature but is rather the gift of divine spirit, a gift given and revealed above all for Paul in the crucified messiah, Jesus of Nazareth, who is sovereign over all worldly powers. It is Paul who gives us the language of "principalities and powers" (*hai archai kai hai exousiai*), and, as G. B. Caird points out in his superb short study,[3] this language pertains to three related domains of reality: politics, religion, and nature—all of which are related to causal language of "law" (*nomos*) of which an account is given by *logos*. The *logos* become flesh provides a different account of the causality of reality, one that (Paul claims) sets us free from the subjugating *nomoi* of worldly powers and authorities that have blinded human eyes to true reality and its (hidden, mysterious) causes. Thus is Critchley also in agreement with Paul, even though he doesn't see this. The question of technology is closely bound up with spiritual vision. This battle of science, religion, and politics continues unabated in our own time, a battle over an account of the true causes of disorder, suffering, and unhappiness in the world and of the true causes by which we might be liberated from those forms of bondage.

With technology, of course, we encounter another *logos* term and, as we know from Aristotle, *techne* as a craft or art is always tied to a *logos* or an account of something—and particular accounts are always related to larger causal accounts of the real. The term *technology* bears witness to this relationship within itself, as Heidegger's famous essay "The Question Concerning Technology" makes profoundly clear.[4] Good practice of these human crafts or arts is related to good *logoi* in what ethicists will call "virtue," by which we simply mean the proper human habituation of "techne"

---

2. See Friedrich Nietzsche, *Anti-Christ*, sec. 47. See my interpretation of Paul and Nietzsche on messianic political philosophy in "Living 'As If Not': Messianic Becoming or the Practice of Nihilism?," in *Paul, Philosophy, and the Theopolitical Vision*, ed. Douglas Harink (Eugene, OR: Cascade, 2010).

3. G. B. Caird, *Principalities and Powers: A Study in Pauline Theology* (1956; reprint, Eugene, OR: Wipf & Stock, 2003).

4. Martin Heidegger, *The Question Concerning Technology and Other Essays*, trans. William Lovitt (New York: Garland, 1977) 3–35.

and "logos" so as to become "strong" human agents and communities—"capable of good judgement/discernment," we might call it, or practical wisdom, *phronesis* (a kind of spiritual vision). Only this, for the ancient Greeks, can offer a hope that leads to happiness, freedom, a well-ordered community in body and soul. Arts or *techne* of the body such as medicine, gymnastics, and cooking require an account of health and its causes; arts or *techne* of the soul such as judging and legislating require an account of justice and its causes. And these accounts will be related. If this is so, and I will assume it is so also for Saint Paul and for Christian hope, we begin to see why religion (or worship) and politics (authority, sovereignty, power) and science (knowledge of the nature of things in the real world) are so closely related.

But as I've said, these relations are also deeply ambiguous and agonistic, as Paul's language of principalities and powers reveals. For Paul, as for Aeschylus and Plato, this agonism and ambiguity requires not merely a mathematical account of order rooted in external quantifying measurement, but a dramatic one—what Heidegger also identifies as language of revelation, a "bringing forth" or a *poiesis*, a spiritual making that is not simply of our own human doing. Furthermore, the question of principalities in the ancient world raises the *political* question of sovereignty and therefore directs us above all to the philosophical and theological *governing* questions, the question of *arche* (Lat.: *princeps*)—the question of beginnings and endings, the de-termining and terminal or "framing" questions, sometimes called foundational. But I simply want to note here again that for Paul and the New Testament those foundational questions are fully dramatic and personal, not codified in doctrinal logics, juridical claims, or ethical systems. An interesting conjunction of the primary words in my title (technology and principality) appears in Paul's self-description in 1 Cor 3:10 where he calls himself a *sophos architekton*, a wise architect, sometimes translated as "skilled master builder," and we might remind ourselves here of Aristotle's designation of the political philosopher as an "architect of the end" (*Ethics* 1.1094b) who builds up happiness and the political good via *phronesis*.[5] Paul's efforts in this regard are devoted to building up (*oikodome*) the body of Christ, as a coworker (*synergos*) with God to build a structure, envisioned as a messianic body whose foundation (*themelios*) is the messianic mind (*phroneite*, Phil 2; cf. the *nous* of 1 Cor 2:16; 1:10). This mind,

---

5. See the discussion by Bruno Blumenfeld, *The Political Paul: Justice, Democracy and Kingship in a Hellenistic Framework*, JSOT 210 (London: Sheffield Academic Press, 2001).

which for Paul is tied to the revelation of the divine mystery (*mysterion*, Lat.: *sacramentum*) that is spiritually/pneumatically, not naturally (and certainly not mechanically!), revealed,[6] is attuned to a wisdom (*sophion*, 1 Cor 2:7) not understood by the *archontes* of this age who are governed by the "spirit of the world" (*to pneuma tou kosmou*, 2:12). Otherwise they would not have crucified the Lord of glory, an act of disincarnation that seeks to eliminate divine mystery from the world so as to control it on their own terms.

Perhaps here we can begin to see how modern technology comes into view as a worldly *archon* of this age, and I want now to attempt a theological and ethical account of this. The topic is of course vast. We could look at current technologies of the body, the ways in which we practice modern medicine, for example, in relation to a contemporary *logos* of health. If we were to do so we might make the argument, as Ivan Illich and Barbara Duden do,[7] that much of modern medicine is practiced in a culture of disincarnation, a denial of the flesh as reflecting divine mystery and a denial of the suffering of the cross as having anything to do with health. Health, indeed, has come to be understood in terms of a global technological "system" or hi-tech systems of "bio-management" into which we are progressively integrated in a manner that disregards and disrespects our "personhood" (a term, we might note, that has come to be increasingly identified in legal terms with economic "corporations," to which our health-care systems are closely tied). Is this good for our (personal or communal) health? Can it heal our diseases or does it proliferate them? Does it console us in our suffering or intensify that suffering? To make a proper theological assessment would require us to interpret clinical rituals (and *techne* always appear in ritual settings) in relation to the whole liturgical practice of medicine and compare this form of worship and authority to the sacramental practice of the eucharist, for example, or the liturgical anointing of the sick or the administration of last rites.

Or, for example, we could examine technologies of the soul, such as the modern practices of justice in what we now call the "criminal justice system." It too has exploded exponentially in the past half-century, as is

---

6. See also Rom 8:5, 27 (*phronema*) and Rom 12:2 (*nous*).

7. Ivan Illich, *Medical Nemesis: The Expropriation of Health* (New York: Pantheon, 1976); Barbara Duden, "The Quest for Past Somatics," in *The Challenges of Ivan Illich: A Collective Reflection*, ed. Lee Hoinacki and Carl Mitcham (Albany: SUNY Press, 2002) 219–30; Duden, *Disembodying Women: Perspectives on Pregnancy and the Unborn*, trans. Lee Hoinacki (Cambridge, MA: Harvard University Press, 1993).

attested to by the enormous sociopolitical and economic investments devoted to its expanding control and maintenance in the building of courts, appointing judges, enhancing and training police, to say nothing of the incredible boom in building and filling prisons in an increasingly "carceral society."[8] Have these new technologies of judgment, discipline, and punishment led to a higher level of social justice and effective practices and institutions that make our communities safer, more peaceful, less violent and disordered? What kinds of virtues have they fostered? The answer to that of course depends on the *logos* of justice that is making judgments about these *techne*. As Dostoevsky already saw in nineteenth-century Russia, the practice of judgement is closely tied to the rituals and liturgies that mediate the *logos* informing the *techne*. As I have argued elsewhere, Dostoevsky's last great novel *The Brothers Karamazov* concerns the political and religious meanings of justice.[9] The radicality in Dostoevsky's contrast between retributive and restorative justice (a justice of wrath and a justice of salvation) is artistically depicted in the two central ritual settings of justice in *Brothers Karamazov*—the monastic cell of Elder Zosima and the modern secular courtroom. It is no accident that the meeting between father and brothers Karamazov to mediate their dispute in the elder's cell early in the novel is a classic Dostoevskyan scandal scene, widely enjoyed for its sacrilegious buffoonery. Less well understood is the profound liturgical expression of spiritual discernment and restorative social justice it represents in the novel as a whole. The by contrast very lengthy and serious justice scene in the final third of the novel (by far the longest scene in a very long novel) is played out in the liturgical setting of the modern Russian courtroom, regarding the crime of parricide that gives the novel its central literal and symbolic dramatic movement. This scene will be taken seriously by readers, as Dostoevsky well knew, because we psychically and culturally "buy" the liturgical structure of the secular courtroom, and we consider its rituals to be endowed with worshipful political and religious authority. We swear solemn oaths to it on a closed Christian Bible. The courtroom, its

---

8. This is Michel Foucault's terminology in *Discipline and Punish: The Birth of the Prison*, trans. Alan Sheridan (New York: Vintage, 1977). For Foucault this techno-social vision is symbolically depicted in the surveillance mechanism of Jeremy Bentham's "panopticon."

9. P. Travis Kroeker, "On the Difference between Torture and Punishment: Theology, Liturgy, and Human Rights," in *Theology, University, Humanities: Initium Sapientiae Timor Domini*, ed. Christopher Craig Brittain and Francesca Aran Murphy (Eugene, OR: Cascade, 2011) 19–38.

liturgy, liturgical players and icons—above all enshrining the sovereign rule of law understood as structuring and protecting the rights of contractual individuals—is the symbolic heart of one of the largest colonizing missions in human history: the global export of modern Western civilization as the model of the highest, happiest, most prosperous and most just form of human life ever attained. Dostoevsky's scandalous claim is that this ritual of retributive justice travesties true messianic justice, and his wager in the novel is that only the monastic disciplines and practices of the messianic community (a "monasticism in the world," the Elder Zosima calls it) will liberate us from the false sovereignty of modern technological desire. Only a messianic materialism will restore to us the divine mystery of our created embodiment, our "personhood." I will return to this.

Cybernetic Technology and Virtual Reality

I want now to move from these specific examples to a consideration of modern cybernetic technologies that have led us to the brink of the most extreme forms of death dealing and depersonalizing disembodiment under the slogan of liberating us from bondage to nature. "Virtual reality," we have come to call it, but it is really a death camp, without smoke stacks—well, at least we think we will eliminate the smoke stacks eventually through technological progress. Here I think we get a glimpse of "the god of this age" (2 Cor 4:4), the "archon of the authority of the air" (Eph 2:2) who blinds the eyes of those who worship the kind of power and the account of nature this principality represents.

What happens when the basic metaphors of nature, including human nature, are reduced to mechanistic process and technical information? I begin with a quotation from the well-known biologist Richard Dawkins: "We are survival machines—robot vehicles blindly programmed to preserve the selfish molecules known as genes. This is a truth which still fills me with astonishment," he gushes.[10] In case there were any doubt that this is no Socratic philosophical wonder (over whether the human being is a monster more complicated and furious than Typhon or a gentler, simpler creature related by nature to the divine [*Phaedrus* 230a]), Dawkins clarifies his remark in his philosophical apologia: "But that was no metaphor. I believe it is the literal truth, provided key words are defined in the particular way favored

---

10. Richard Dawkins, *The Selfish Gene* (London: Granada, 1978) ix.

by biologists."[11] This of course makes us curious about the favored linguistic preferences of biologists; as it stands, it seems an astonishing reductionism. Not only does it attribute a single moral intentionality (selfishness no less!) to the whole of life. It also uncritically names us "survival machines" or "robot vehicles," which one should have thought are strange metaphors for a biologist to choose. And yet it is not uncommon. For biologists human nature has become revealed as techno-genetic standing reserves.

Dr. Robert Haynes, president of the 16th International Congress of Genetics (Yale, 1988), states,

> For three thousand years at least, a majority of people have considered that human beings were special. . . . It's the Judeo-Christian view of man. What the ability to manipulate genes should indicate to people is the very deep extent to which we are biological machines. The traditional view is built on the foundation that life is sacred. . . . Well, not anymore. It's no longer possible to live by the idea that there is something special, unique, even sacred about living organisms.[12]

Machines, of course, are humanly made, artificial, engineered, usually not as a display of beauty or spiritual identity, but as instruments—usually of control or procurement. Is it surprising that the *techne* of our culture take on machinelike attributes when our primary metaphors are mechanistic? Increasingly not only our industrial economy but also our politics and our aesthetics take on the features of our primary linguistic metaphors, which are of course closely tied to a *logos*. Why else would people spend all that time and energy to make themselves look like the very muscle-building machinery they use to get them there? Why else are our lucrative fashion industries successfully marketing the hairless, well-oiled, "enhanced" body except that we literally are coming to see ourselves not as animal creatures but increasingly as biomechanical machines? Cyborgs? And of course who wouldn't be willing to become a machine if it means avoiding a human death? The future markets in the cosmetic, therapeutic, and functional enhancement of the human machine (indeed, the "nature machine") are vast indeed—and a great deal of research is being funded to exploit these opportunities as central values in our public culture. To what extent is our techno-science guided by a morally laden *logos* of nature that denies its

---

11. Dawkins, "In Defence of Selfish Genes," *Philosophy* 56 (1981) 572.

12. As quoted in Andrew Kimbrell, *The Human Body Shop: The Cloning, Engineering, and Marketing of Life*, 2nd ed. (Washington, DC: Regnery, 1997) 283.

own moral judgments and assumptions as such (by assuming the mechanistic metaphor is objective rational description)? Of course, machines are not moral agents; hence if we are machines, are we moral agents? Or just power systems? Do we have a soul that is anything more than a ghost in the machine? Is the effort to enhance our machinelike efficiency a moral enterprise and, if so, what is the good it seeks and how will we speak about it?

In order to explore this question, the good of technological research and development, we do well to examine the cultural-linguistic (*logos*) history of modern science and its intimate connections with technology and the mechanistic paradigm.[13] As Carolyn Merchant's aptly titled book *The Death of Nature* argues, the modern vision of science has been closely tied to certain Baconian moral assumptions, most notably the commitment to relieve and benefit the human condition by liberating human beings from the constraints of nature, and delivering control of nature, including human nature, into human hands.[14] "Knowledge is power," said Bacon, and by this he meant the power to *generate*, a power closely linking scientific research and technical development.[15] Bacon scoffed at the wisdom of the classical moral traditions and their language of the good, comparing it to prepubescent boyhood: "it can talk, but it cannot generate" (*Magna Instauratio*, Preface). It is worth paying some attention to this language of "generating," since etymologically it is linked to an important family of words in our public culture: *genius, engine/engineer, gene/genetic*—all linked to the Latin *gigno/gignere*, to beget, and the Greek *gignomai*, to be born/come into being. That is to say, it is language closely linked to central motives in a *logos* about *arche* as "origin," causality, bringing into being.

---

13. We could do the same with politics and political theory, beginning with Hobbes' *Leviathan*. What Bacon did for modern science Hobbes did for modern politics with his image of the great Leviathan as the gigantic, artificial, mechanistic "human being writ large" that represents the body politic stripped of all spiritual causality. I have attempted a brief account of this in "Messianic Ethics and Diaspora Communities: Upbuilding the Secular Theologically from Below," in *Religious Voices in Public Places*, ed. Nigel Biggar and Linda Hogan (Oxford: Oxford University Press, 2009) 110–30.

14. Carolyn Merchant, *The Death of Nature: Women, Ecology, and the Scientific Revolution* (New York: Harper & Row, 1980) ch. 7. For her updated argument in the face of a spate of critical literature, see "The Violence of Impediments: Francis Bacon and the Origins of Experimentation," *Isis* 99 (2008) 731–60.

15. "*ipsa scientia potestas est,*" said Bacon in *Meditationes Sacrae* (1597), by which he was referring to divine creative power, related to his hope that science would enable human beings to restore the godlike power to dominate nature lost in the fall (*Novum Organon*, Book 2). Hobbes reduces this to "*scientia potentia est,*" in contrast to the more traditional "*sapientia est potentia,*" in *Leviathan* 1.10.

- *Genius*: classically, the tutelary or attendant spirit allotted to every person (or place or institution) at birth, influencing it for good or evil as that which gives moral form to the desires, the passions—that which we seek or love. Our coming into being is not only into a biological, but also a spiritual and moral begetting, by which our character or spirit or dispositions are shaped. Increasingly in the modern context, "genius" comes to be identified with inventive talent and technical ability of an externalized kind.

- *Engine/Engineer* (from Lat., *ingenium/ingeniator*—linked to genius): traditionally referred to a natural quality, a person's disposition and moral character—that which *moves* a person: attitudes, pursuits, aims. In modern times, as we know, this is increasingly given a purely instrumental meaning and technical skill, to the point that the traditional meaning has disappeared. "Engines" are now mechanisms of external motion and engineers are those professionals who design efficient machines that generate desired motions. It is, in effect, closely tied to technological power—as a profession, of course, "engineering" originated in a military context as the design and operation of engines of war and was until the end of the eighteenth century primarily a military career. The nineteenth and twentieth centuries saw the rapid expansion of civil engineering in the service of public works and then increasingly commercial enterprises—viewed as the engines of human liberation and control over nature and destiny.[16] In the late twentieth and twenty-first centuries engineering becomes intimately tied to the biomedical and information technologies, the latest locus of our hopes for human liberation and happiness.

- *Gene/genetic*: units of heredity and biological transmission that shape the characteristics of offspring. Originally defined as ultimate units of mutation and recombination, they are now defined as sequences of DNA—increasingly described in images taken from the cybernetic and information sciences. It is, I suppose, not surprising that the instrument used to discover the DNA double helix—the computer—inspired the imagery of the new biology. Watson and Crick referred to the helix structure of the gene as a "code, programmed with chemical

---

16. Herbert Hoover was the first civil engineer President of the United States. Of course, lest we forget, Adolf Eichmann was also an engineer by profession and became highly proficient in the engineering of death camps—he considered himself, as his primary defense in his trial, to be simply "following orders" of his superiors.

information to be deciphered."[17] The "cracking" of the genetic code, which will unlock the secrets of life, is a massive computational exercise in information processing.

Rather than focus here on particular ethical issues that are raised by this language and the action it generates—patenting of genetic information as intellectual property, the moral ambiguities entailed in various forms of genetic testing, cloning, and the new benevolent eugenics entailed in the biotech revolution that increasingly funds so much research in the life and health sciences—I want to consider the moral consequences of the shifts in language that I've briefly sketched. What happens when basic biological nature comes to be seen as information, and organisms as information-processing machines whose capacities can be progressively upgraded into increasingly efficient cybernetic survival systems?

I begin with Francis Bacon's own thought experiment envisioning the future of modern scientific civilization in his utopic *New Atlantis*. The *New Atlantis* culminates in a vision of benevolent scientific empire communicated by the father of wise Solomon's House (a.k.a. the "College of Six Days' Work" instituted for the production of marvelous scientific works for human benefit), who comes in secret to give Bacon his blessing at a private conference. He states, "The end of our foundation is the knowledge of causes and secret motions of things; and the enlarging of the bounds of human empire, to the effecting of all things possible."[18] Thereupon follows a vision of technological empire that masters all of nature, including human nature, through a vast artificial infrastructure by which nature is subordinated to instrumental control—an order that respects not beauty but efficiency, says the father. It is a stunningly prescient vision: of novel plant species fashioned without seeds or natural generation, elaborate and extensive animal dissections and experiments that change them beyond species boundaries via artificial generation, an astonishing array of medicinal drugs and mechanical arts and penetrating diagnostic instruments. The last of the scientific powers listed are "houses of deceits of the senses," where the miracles of virtual reality are displayed—though of course as good scientists, the moral father hastens to add, "we do hate all impostures and lies" amongst fellow scientists who hold the power in this empire so

---

17. Quoted in Jeremy Rifkin, *The Biotech Century: Harnessing the Gene and Remaking the World* (New York: Putnam, 1998) 181.

18. Francis Bacon, *The Advancement of Learning and New Atlantis* (London: Oxford University Press, 1951) 288.

that to one another only nature "pure as it is, and without all affectation of strangeness" will be displayed.[19]

However, the question here quickly becomes, what are the "pure truths" of nature and what are mere conceits or dangerous deceits in the house of scientific culture? If nature is merely an information code to be cracked so that its various data may be reconfigured in endless different patterns, how might we distinguish true from false, benevolent from malevolent, healthy from harmful experiments, innovations, and developments? If there is no "good" in nature, including no moral goodness that can be commonly discerned, why even bother with ethics in scientific research and technological innovation?

I conclude this section with reference to another vision of technological empire as "posthumanism" that has in effect eliminated embodiment altogether—this one current and very influential right now in North American public life, represented here by Ray Kurzweil's *Age of Spiritual Machines*.[20] Kurzweil is no flake; his work in artificial intelligence and pattern recognition technologies has led to the successful establishment of four high-tech companies (devoted, among other things, to pattern recognition technologies that aid the blind and the deaf), a number of influential books, and a host of academic and other national and international awards, including the U.S. National Medal of Technology (awarded him in 1999 by President Clinton). He is in many ways an icon of our culture's commercial and research aspirations, his books are the preferred reading of the political and business (and I suspect also certain academic) elites both in the United States and Canada.[21]

What is Kurzweil's vision? In a nutshell it is this: "Computation is the essence of order" (33). The evolutionary process that has begotten human intelligence is effectively generating an increasingly efficient information-processing machine. Kurzweil is convinced that human beings are the intermediate organic stage toward a new, essentially cybernetic technological stage of evolutionary development in which machine technology will

---

19. Ibid., 296.

20. Ray Kurzweil, *The Age of Spiritual Machines: When Computers Exceed Human Intelligence* (New York: Penguin, 1999). Further references appear by page number in parentheses.

21. Compare also the work of another such "visionary," UCLA biophysicist Gregory Stock, in his books *Metaman: The Merging of Humans and Machines into a Global Superorganism* (New York: Simon & Schuster, 1993), and *Redesigning Humans: Our Inevitable Genetic Future* (Boston: Houghton Mifflin, 2002).

eventually "take full control of its own progression" (32). This is indeed what human intelligence and consciousness really is, after all, when we get past "hard-to-define questions such as human dignity" (57). While the Human Genome Project is important as a scanning operation of DNA codes, it will ultimately be superseded by machine intelligence, according to what Kurzweil calls the "Law of Accelerating Returns," which interprets all reality on the model of increasingly complex information processing. What this means is that for intelligent organisms to adapt themselves to a changing natural—read "machine"—environment, in order to keep up with the evolutionary processes and maintain their evolutionary advantage, human beings will of necessity turn themselves into machines, gradually at first through genetic therapies, bio-enhancement and porting our brains to computer intelligence. But eventually we will have to realize that "DNA-based evolution will eventually have to be abandoned" because "organisms created through DNA-based evolution are stuck with an extremely plodding type of circuitry" (101). Kurzweil's vision ends with the claim that "extremely little of the stuff on Earth is devoted to useful computation. This is even more true when we consider all of the dumb matter in the Earth's midst" (259). The aim of all life is to exploit nature for its computational intelligence (which is what Kurzweil means by "spirituality"), which will transform life into a shared machine consciousness, a posthuman virtual reality, where all things are possible—without God.

Kurzweil's book is filled with examples of what may be achieved through this bio-technological (and commercial) revolution, which he describes as "a road paved with gold . . . full of benefits that we're never going to resist" (130). For example, he is fond of speculating on the sexual possibilities that will open up when freed from the constraints of biological generation and conventional social norms. Sexual and spiritual activities can be reduced to information processing, not complex personal relations sustained through time or in nature, not educated through suffering and challenge and disciplined commitments between persons. Sex is merely the episodic manipulation of electronic data. Kurzweil finds it in him to celebrate the technological possibilities of virtual sex of every kind, which will no longer require moral censure because now safely detached from the constraints of embodied nature. He imagines his fourth-grade son's ability to undress his fourth-grade teacher—and manipulate her in any way he desires—without affecting *her*; he imagines the ability to indulge many lovers at once, pleasuring himself by clicking on innumerable sites and partners at the same time (though I suppose eventually no real clicking will be required). So too the spiritual arts (music, poetry, painting) can easily be replicated by computer technology, and unfortunately Kurzweil cannot restrain himself from giving examples of his own design—all I can say is that if you love poetry and art, don't go there. The commodities on offer are at about the same level of moral wisdom and emotional intelligence as the fourth-grade sexual fantasies. We are now literally generating ("safe"!) sex for prepubescent boys, who no longer need either to talk or to generate.

How is it that our human quest for liberation and happiness ends up in such a tawdry and dehumanizing vision of totalitarian, mechanistic disembodiment—one that is nevertheless celebrated as the benevolent salvation of the future? I suggest it has something to do with the fact that we think we will magically crack the code of life through the collection of data. This is a Faustian bargain. Data lacks sanctity and goodness; to be sure it takes attention away from our moral and spiritual sensibilities, which are developed and communicated through a different sort of language—the language of symbol, narrative and the ordering of love, justice, beauty, and goodness. This classical moral language is attuned to a different kind of knowing than is the instrumental procurement and processing of data, and it is important to recognize this philosophically if we are to preserve a shared rational language (*logos*) that discloses to us spiritually and culturally who we truly are.

Now of course this reference to the spiritual raises the specter of pluralism. Especially in our so-called global culture there are many different traditions—religious, moral, philosophical—that try to tell us who we are or ought to be. Which one will we choose to guide our scientific and technological decisions? By now I hope you will anticipate at least the first part of my answer, namely, not by trying to find a single system or linguistic moral code that will sort out all possible conflicts and problems. Part of the problem in secular technological society is that we have sought precisely such solutions—another technical procedure, be it law or medicine or organizational theory. As T. S. Eliot says of modern human beings in "Choruses from 'The Rock'" (VI):

> They constantly try to escape
> From the darkness outside and within
> By dreaming of systems so perfect that no one will need to be good.
> But the man that is will shadow
> The man that pretends to be . . .

What we need in the first place, rather, is an account of spiritual causality, if I may put it this way, in the language of poetic, dramatic experience, a return to our personhood—which is particular, limited, embodied, passing away and yet inhabited, indeed inspired, by divine mystery.

The Messianic Annihilation/Reconciliation of "All Things"

How then are human beings to find life again in the midst of these disembodying and death-dealing principalities? I suggest it will require a liberation from the pervasive language of "responsibility" in our public ethics. This is a language closely tied to worldly power, the power to control reality in a manner that overcomes the vulnerability of contingency, embodied particularity, and spiritual mystery.[22] Language of responsibility is closely tied to the juridical codes of professional ethics, to which even an Adolf Eichmann could appeal with his "*Nicht schuldig*"—I was simply following professional orders and doing my responsible duty as one called upon to engineer the most efficient death camps possible. For the Apostle Paul too, the principalities and powers are closely correlated with juridical codes and legal dogmas—which are of no avail, he says, in liberating human beings from bondage to their false authority (Col 2:20–23). I note here that not only the *techne* of professional ethics but also the *techne* of religious authorities oriented toward control based on the possession of human knowledge have the effect, for Paul, of sinful disincarnation (1 Cor 8). They destroy rather than build up the body for which Christ died, a body rooted in the mystery of divine incarnation, suffering, death, and resurrection. This mystery only comes into view, we might say, through the *techne* of sacramental practices—*sacramentum* being the Latin term for the Greek word *mysterion*. This body, furthermore, includes "all things," all created reality that seeks its divine completion.

We should note that for Paul this word *mysterion* can also be used with reference to the "mystery of iniquity" (2 Thess 2:7f.), the *parousia* of *anomia* (iniquity or "lawlessness") associated with Satan, and enacted with deceptively powerful "signs and wonders." The messianic *parousia* and the

---

22. See the following essays by Carl Mitcham: "Technology and the Burden of Responsibility," in *Values and Ethics for the 21st Century*, ed. F. Gonzalez et al. (Madrid: BBVA, 2012) 141–66; and "Responsibility and Technology: The Expanding Relationship," in *Technology and Responsibility*, ed. Paul T. Durbin (Boston: D. Reidel, 1987) 3–39. See also Ivan Illich, *The Rivers North of the Future* (Toronto: House of Anansi, 2005) ch. 21.

satanic *parousia* are "apocalypsed" together. As Ivan Illich points out,[23] the mystery of this evil revealed in the heavenly places (as "Antichrist") is the corruption of the best, which happens when the incarnational "Gospel" is falsely institutionalized and turned into yet another universalizing global system that claims to bring salvation. This is precisely a betrayal of the intimate truth of the embodied kenotic gospel, and it leads to the attempt to curse God's incarnation (even when it "blesses"). It builds up human empire in false godlikeness, in Babel-like fashion reducing culture to a single language, a univocal naming of reality "in order to make a name for ourselves" over against God. By contrast we note the "having become" (*genesthai* and its variants [1 Thess 1:6, 7])[24] in which Paul is yoked together with the Thessalonians by receiving the apocalyptic word "in much affliction" and yet "with spiritual joy" (1:6).[25] For Paul this "becoming," this enactment of the truly human messianic body is rooted in a "turning-around" (1:9) away from idols to serve "a living and true God, and to wait for his Son from heaven." But this waiting is not mere passivity related to "times and seasons" (5:1) of some future event. It is an entering into the "affliction" of the present time, the birthing of messianic love in the midst of false, destructive forms of "peace and security" (5:3f.). For Paul this is not an otherworldly hope, but the enactment of a hope that takes place in quiet, embodied service of others in everyday life (4:11).[26]

The demonic perversion of truth, as Ivan Illich shows, is not simply a violation of the laws of reality but a personal turning away from an intimate revelation of divine reality in whose image human beings are created. Its correlative is a turning in worship toward a false substitute, the apostatic *mysterium iniquitatis* Paul speaks about in 2 Thessalonians 2,[27] revealed as

23. Illich, *Rivers North*, ch. 2.

24. See the penetrating interpretation by Martin Heidegger in his early work on Paul, *The Phenomenology of Religious Life*, trans. Matthias Fritsch and Jennifer Anna Gosetti-Ferencei (Bloomington: Indiana University Press, 2004) 47–111.

25. The Apostle Paul describes the intimacy of this union in "having become" when he says "in all our distress and affliction we have been comforted about you through your faith; for now *we live, if you stand fast* in the Lord" (1 Thess 3:7–8). See also his strong language, where "having become" is linked to Jesus's messianic "coming" (*parousia*) in 1 Thess 2:8, 19–20; 3:11–13.

26. In my article "Messianic Ethics and Diaspora Communities" (see note 13 above) I contrast "diaspora ethics" in the everyday to the globalizing ethics of Leviathan-Babel-empire.

27. Illich, *Rivers North*, chs. 2, 14. Here is one of Illich's pithy formulations of what he means: "The Anti-Christ, or, let's say, the *mysterium iniquitatis*, the mystery of evil, is the

anti-Messiah in the apocalypse of Messiah and as characterized by mendacious power and wicked deception. This is the personal, intimate character of sin that also has pervasive social and political consequences—the substitution of other-regarding personal love by self-securing institutional power. It may also be described as a turn away from the divine Spirit of love enfleshed in the person of Jesus toward a trust once again in the juridical, institutional constraints of external rules and codes of behavior—a shift from a community rooted in "con-spiratio" (personal faith, love, sin, forgiveness inspired by the divine Spirit) to one rooted in "con-juratio" (the juridical state structure).[28] The impersonal, instrumental and juridical character of modern social and political ethics, related to risk assessment and technical requirements of security systems (be they legal, educational or medical), are the shared consequences of this shift in spiritual vision.

Let us return to the question of hope. In 1 Cor 15:24–28 Paul ties hope in resurrection with the messianic *katargesis* of every principality and power in a passage in which "all" or "all things" (*pan/pantes/ta panta*) occurs ten times. The word *katargesis* is sometimes translated destruction or "annihilation." Paul uses the same verb in 1 Cor 1:28 with reference to the wisdom and power of the cross: God chooses the things without being (*ta me onta*) to bring to nothing (*katargese*) the things with being (*ta onta*). What does this mean, and how are cross and resurrection brought together in this verb that disarms the principalities and powers by setting aside their power to hold creation in the bonds of death (Col 1–2)? And how is it that through this agency of suffering the Messiah now in his enfleshed body reconciles a sinful, divided and death-dealing creation with God? For Paul this is a divine mystery, one disclosed above all in the emptying movement of kenosis hymned in Philippians 2. It begins, of course, with God becoming enfleshed in the body of a young woman who accepts the begetting of her child as miraculous divine gift, and also a gift of suffering and mortality, that requires her kenosis, her self-emptying.

---

conglomerate of a series of perversions by which we try to give security, survival ability, and independence from individual persons to the new possibilities that were opened through the Gospel by institutionalizing them" (169). Compare Augustine's reflection on 2 Thess 2 and the possible meaning of the *Antichristo* as the "universal body" of the prince of apostasy, standing over against the messianic body as lie against truth (*City of God* 20.19). I have attempted an extended interpretation in "Augustine's Messianic Political Theology: An Apocalyptic Critique of Political Augustinianism," in *Augustine and Apocalyptic*, ed. John Doody et al., Augustine in Conversation: Tradition and Innovation (Lanham, MD: Lexington, 2014) 129–49.

28. Illich, *Rivers North*, chs. 5, 15, 16.

Let me suggest in conclusion that this incarnational, personal technological vision is perhaps most importantly depicted for Paul in his experience of the resurrected crucified messiah (which is where we began), an experience made visible in the sacraments, the embodied worship of the messianic suffering servant. This worship entails a sacrificial posture that breaks down dividing walls of hostility based on nature (male/female), religion (Jew/Greek), and sociopolitical status (slave/free), the three related domains of principalities mentioned by Caird. In proclaiming this hope Paul was quite aware of its scandalous claims with regard to visible human authority. In his famous address to the Athenians (Acts 17:16f.) Paul relates the teaching that all human beings are generated by the divine as God's offspring to the teaching about the resurrection of the body. The resurrection is the vindication of the mystery of divine incarnation as dispossessive, kenotic, and it is celebrated in the sacrament of this enfleshment—not only a ritual liturgical event but also that which is liturgically enacted in all the *techne* of charity. As the Elder Zosima proclaims, active love, unlike love in dreams rooted in isolated fantasies, is hard work requiring daily unglorious, ascetic perseverance.[29] It enters into affliction, with joy. It requires death to the self-desiring ego in order to be reborn in the "one mind" of messianic kinship where in humility we work to build up communities in our shared mortal flesh.

We know from his diaries on *The Brothers Karamazov* that Dostoevsky worried mightily that the monastic path of the Elder Zosima would not provide a compelling response to Ivan's techno-religious, demonic vision of the Grand Inquisitor in the novel. The current teaching of the world, says the elder, is the gratification and expansion of one's desires:

> For you have the same rights as the noblest and richest men. . . . But what comes of this right to increase one's needs? For the rich, *isolation* and spiritual suicide; for the poor, envy and murder, for they have been given rights, but have not yet been shown any way of satisfying their needs. We are assured that the world is becoming more and more united, is being formed into brotherly

---

29. Fyodor Dostoevsky, *The Brothers Karamazov*, trans. Richard Pevear and Larissa Volokhonsky (New York: Vintage, 1990). "I am sorry that I cannot say anything more comforting, for active love is a harsh and fearful thing compared with love in dreams. Love in dreams thirsts for immediate action, quickly performed, and with everyone watching. . . . Whereas active love is labor and perseverance, and for some people, perhaps, a whole science" (58)—a *techne*, we might say. "Brothers, love is a teacher, but one must know how to acquire it, for it is difficult to acquire, it is dearly bought, by long work over a long time . . ." (319).

communion, by the shortening of distances, by the transmitting of thoughts through the air [remember, this is being written in the mid-nineteenth century!]. Alas, do not believe in such a union of people. Taking freedom to mean the increase and prompt satisfaction of needs, they distort their own nature, for they generate many meaningless and foolish desires, habits, and the most absurd fancies in themselves. They live only for mutual envy, for pleasure-seeking and self-display.[30]

By contrast the elder articulates the monastic way: "Obedience, fasting, and prayer are laughed at, yet they constitute the way to real and true freedom: I cut away my superfluous and unnecessary needs, through obedience I humble and chasten my vain and proud will, and thereby, with God's help, attain freedom of spirit, and with that, spiritual rejoicing!"[31] Only one freed from the isolation of self-love can truly love others, and such freedom is made possible through spiritual rebirth in the image of Christ—conformity to the "form of the servant" that builds up the human community through embodied deeds of humble love.

---

30. Ibid., 313–14. For extended discussion, see P. Travis Kroeker and Bruce K. Ward, *Remembering the End: Dostoevsky as Prophet to Modernity* (Boulder, CO: Westview, 2001) chs. 4 and 6.

31. Dostoyevsky, *Brothers Karamazov*, 314.

www.ingramcontent.com/pod-product-compliance
Lightning Source LLC
Chambersburg PA
CBHW032232080426
42735CB00008B/824